Exposed

Memoirs of an Exotic Dancer

C. B. Haley

This book is memoir.

It reflects the author's recollections of the events.

It discusses drug use and sexual content. Discretion advised.

Names of individuals have been changed to protect the privacy of all those involved.

The stories are all true.

© 2022 C. B. Haley

Hazy Reflections

"Are you okay?" one of the bouncers asked me with a concerned look on his face. I had just stumbled out of one of the private dance rooms in the club. I nodded my head signifying that I was fine, although the honest answer would have been far more complicated than that. I made my way down the stairs and through the dark hallway that followed, arriving in the bathroom. I looked in the reflection and barely recognized myself in my coked-out haze.

Like a Moth to a Flame

I've always been drawn to the darkness. I've longed for experiences that exist beyond the norm of society. I think some people are just like that. There's intrigue in the taboo, within the fringes of society. Perhaps it's as simple as a deep boredom; a restlessness that seems insatiable.

I wish I could explain how I got there, but the truth is, I can't decipher one specific moment that led me to that place. I've always been drawn to intensity; lives that are messy, complicated, raw — and often, characters who are self-destructive. Without admitting this point, I'd be disregarding a massive part of my own personality that attracted me to the lifestyle.

More than anything, I think I wanted to rebel.

I'm a middle child who, like many others, has always tried desperately to forge my own path. In university I studied Sociology and English, and if nothing else, I feel I gained the ability to question the way our society functions. I felt I was trying to fight against the sexism that is so deeply ingrained within it. But in doing so, I somehow lost my way and became a part of it by infiltrating the fringes.

Even now, years after the fact, I'm not sure I've gained clear insight into whether stripping is inherently negative or whether it can be a lighthearted, fun night out. I've made friendships with coworkers and customers alike that have had a positive impact that will last my lifetime. For that I am grateful.

I've also witnessed a dark, bleak, and selfish side of humanity, devoid of empathy and love. It's the reason many strippers say they hate men. I can understand that sentiment and the cynical perspective that many exotic dancers develop after years in this industry. It's the reason I had to get out before it consumed my soul and my optimism for kindness amongst humans.

There's a lot of shame that I now carry with me, burdening me and weighing me down. A self-inflicted pain, invisible baggage that I constantly tow behind me into every new experience, with every new person I encounter. I have deep regret, confusion, and ultimately more questions than answers.

Thoughts of the American Dream

I remember that in one of my English courses in university, we studied Chris McCandless, perhaps better known as Alexander Supertramp. He was the inspiration behind the novel and movie Into the Wild, which documented his nomadic lifestyle. He had everything that we're told we should want, the "American Dream": money, an education, a career… Yet he donated his money, cut up his credit cards, and left his previous life behind him in search of something more, journeying into the bush of Alaska.

There's something intangible that people seek to add to their lives. I don't know if I find it comforting that so many of us feel this emptiness within our souls, a desire to find a deeper meaning to our existence. But in some way, it's nice to know that I'm not alone in that feeling. I don't want to be old and look back at my life, reminiscing and feel like I missed out. The worst feeling in the world is feeling like you're sleepwalking through life, merely existing rather than really living.

Chris wasn't the first to do what he did — throw caution to the wind, and really live — and he won't be the last. There are many documented cases, and I would bet infinitely more unknown, where people have attained the goals that we're taught will bring us happiness, only to say that they have a longing for more. Many of us dream of an existence where we live amongst nature in harmony, rather than trying to control it. I didn't go quite that far, but I chose to throw caution to the wind in my own way. I shed the skin of my previous self and entered a world that was entirely foreign to me, disregarding all of the beliefs I'd internalized over the previous twenty-three years.

After completing five years of postgraduate school, I was hoping to find a job within the specific field I studied, Human Resources. I didn't go into this particular program because any aspects of the job itself sounded appealing, but rather because I'd researched careers that were in demand, stable, and decently paying. Like many of my Millenial peers, my parents raised me to believe that the proper path to a successful future was through post-secondary education. I was then supposed to find a career that would support me for the rest of my working days. I'd meet and marry my partner, have 1.9 children, and finally retire with minimal bumps along the way. This was the only trajectory that made sense. The trouble is, everyone else was raised to believe that they too would follow this path to the American Dream (it's still called the American Dream for Canadians, right?), meaning that a post-graduate education was now the equivalent of a high school diploma.

Besides all of the external forces preventing me from attaining the simplest of things on this list — a job — I was also battling some inner conflict. In the year I graduated from my Human Resources program, I lost an uncle. I had known very little about him, besides the fact that he was a brilliant man, entirely selfless, who had dedicated his life to medicine. While easing others' ailments, he himself had been suffering his whole life from a genetic disease that had progressively crushed his quality of life. I then lost my great-nanny, my father's grandmother, who was in her nineties at the time. She was survived by her husband, also in his nineties, who still loved her deeply at the time of her passing. I lost my grandfather, on my mother's side, who had been battling cancer for many years. He was a man with a grandiose presence. He drank hard, he laughed hard, and he argued with anyone about anything just for the hell of it. I'd never truly experienced loss before that year and was left sad and confused.

Only Love

At university, I lived with five other girls in an old, dilapidated house. We were often asked by other students how we managed to get along. "That's too much estrogen under one roof," they'd say, and we'd laugh, because our friendships were effortless. Somehow our personalities, though all drastically different from one another, fit together like puzzle pieces. We complemented one another in every way; I remember a time at our neighbours' party when I sat on their couch beside one of my housemates, Sarah. We'd each had a couple of drinks and stood up, suddenly feeling the effects of the alcohol. "Whoa, guess that's it for me for the night!" Sarah declared. At the same time, I'd just been thinking to myself, Time to get more drinks! My housemates truly brought out the best in me. Those years were some of the happiest of my life, and although I was stressed by assignments, exams, and the ever-looming reality that I didn't know what my future held, I was at peace.

One of the girls I lived with was in the Nursing program. She was completing her clinical placement on campus at the children's hospital, as well as working at a local nursing home. One evening as we sat together in our living room, she told us about one of her elderly patients who was always positive, despite the difficulties she'd endured and the loved ones she'd lost. My housemate had asked her what the secret to life was. The lady had responded, "Love."

A couple of years later, after I'd moved away, I received a text message from one of my university housemates. She told me that our Nursing housemate had died. Our old friend had been hiking with a group of close friends when they stopped to document the experience with a photo in front of a waterfall. The wind brought a tree down from above. The others managed to step back, but she died on the spot.

It didn't make any sense; she wasn't old, she wasn't sick. She was vivacious, caring, and generous. Through this loss, all of the previous deaths somehow compounded and mattered more.

There's no reason for a loss like this. There's no sense in trying to look for one.

I will forever be grateful for her presence in my life, and for the lesson she shared with me: that the meaning of life is love.

Fleeing or Freeing?

I took to running, not in the graceful way that you've probably witnessed real runners do, but in a damaged way. I ran through tall grass in trails near my house that were rarely used, leaping to escape a demon that was nipping at my heels. I was running from reality; from the expectations I felt were placed on me to get a career, a house, and a family of my own. I was running away from the American Dream, and I was hoping to find answers.

I completed an HR contract job that I'd agreed to take on that summer. It was a strange summer full of loneliness and questions. At the end of the season I moved back to my hometown. On a night out drinking with a couple of my girlfriends, one of my best friends from high school, Anna, suggested that we travel to Australia. Her aunt and cousins lived there, she explained, so we could stay with her aunt while we searched for our own apartment.

What began as a fun idea over drinks ended up quite quickly becoming an actual plan for the two of us. Our other friends decided not to join us on our adventure overseas, but Anna and I were all in. It gave me something to look forward to. At that point I was unemployed, feeling lost and without purpose. I clung to the idea of our trip to Australia.

The process began. Anna and I got our Working Holiday Visas, which would allow us to stay in the country for a full year with the possibility of extending, thanks to our Commonwealth status. To be honest, I would have been too scared to venture out on my own, but the thought of having Anna by my side made it more exciting than intimidating. In the following months, we bought our one-way plane tickets and decided that we would be visiting Anna's university friends along the way. One of them lived in Shanghai, and one in Hong Kong. The plan, I was told, was to stay about four days in Shanghai, and then another four days in Hong Kong, before finally arriving at our destination in Melbourne.

Honest Thieves

In a world full of people trying to take from you, greed runs rampant. Corporations claim to care about social justice issues just so that people are persuaded to buy whatever it is that they're selling. Women are supposed to enjoy the Dove "Real Beauty" Campaign where other "regular" women (who are not typically models) share the revelation that we all have flaws… Yet the same company sells "Fair and Lovely," a cream intended to bleach your skin in order to lighten it. What is wrong with this picture?

Perhaps the most honest people in such a world are the ones doing straightforward transactions, like the brothel workers who are under no pretense that people are paying them for any other reason than their bodies. People can say what they want, but when's the last time you were that genuine?

Unhinged

After losing my friend when she was in her early twenties, I was perplexed. At first I was angry, but then I became more confused than anything. Why was it that someone who enjoyed life to the fullest was robbed of time, when someone like me, who often wanted to disappear, was perfectly fine? Damn, I thought, I always knew life was unfair. Turns out death is, too.

Fleeing to the furthest possible part of the world seemed like a good idea at the time. I wanted to get away from everything I knew. It seems that we learn the most when we're thrown into the unknown. I wanted nothing more than to be thrown.

Third Grade

I have a distinct memory of the day in third grade when Edward asked me to date him. He had curly auburn locks, and was a friend of mine. Though flattered, I had no interest in him. I had my eyes on another boy, Caleb, who had a mysterious air about him, bouncing slightly as he walked. That mystery was the appeal.

Edward asked me to be his girlfriend while we were outside at recess. He then tried to present me with candies that he'd purchased at the corner store, using his weekly allowance. It didn't sit well with me. It felt as though he was saying he could buy me. I politely declined the candies, explaining that I didn't want gifts. My mother had raised me, one of three daughters, with the firm belief that I should never rely on a man. I was fully capable of becoming successful on my own, and could in fact save up my own allowance to buy myself candy.

A week later Edward was dating Heather, who had no problem accepting the candy he gave her.

The Journey

Anna and I celebrated Christmas at home with our respective families before flying out on our adventure. We'd decided to leave a couple of days later, on December 27th.

The initial flight took us from a small airport in Waterloo, Ontario to Chicago, Illinois, where we were to board a large jet en route to Shanghai. Despite the ungodly hour at which we arose, leaving our homes before sunrise, we were brimming with energy. I tried to sleep on the plane, but I was too jittery, and only managed to shut my eyes for short periods of time. The rest of my life in reach.

Shanghai

I didn't have a clear image of what China would look like, other than bustling. Shanghai did not disappoint in this regard. If you get claustrophobic, it's not the place for you, but I, for whatever reason, love getting lost in a crowd. It doesn't matter who you are, where you're coming from, or where you're going; in a crowd, everyone is a small moving part of something larger than themselves.

Sophie met us at the airport, greeting us with smiles and hugs. I'd met her a number of times in our university days. She had a way of making you feel at ease, and I forgot for the time being that I was third-wheeling in a foreign country. We hopped in a cab and sped down the highway, veering dangerously onto round interchanges six or so lanes wide. I'd never seen highways like this, or experienced driving where I was thrown about the vehicle in such a way. The driver seemed confident, though.

"Uhh, this is a bit crazy!" Anna commented.

"This is how they drive here!" Sophie informed us, laughing as we flailed around our seats at every lane change and sharp turn.

Sometimes when you're dropped into a culture so drastically different from your own, it takes you out of your own head and places you back into your body. That was my experience in Shanghai. It almost hit a reset button, where I wasn't focused on the past events and instead looked towards the new experiences. The new cuisine, scenery, smells and language all around me: these were good things for me.

New Year's Eve

We were going to be celebrating New Year's Eve in Shanghai. Sophie had arranged for us to all go to a party in a fancy hotel. Some of her friends were renting a room, and we were invited to drink and mingle.

As we walked into the entrance of the hotel, the grand entryway took our breath away. Since I'm almost 5'9, it was the first time I'd felt small since we'd arrived in Shanghai. The floor was marble, and the walls were dark, but a massive chandelier illuminated our way. Everything felt magnificent, and I felt a bit like a traitor. Like I was pretending to be someone I wasn't.

The night itself ended up being uneventful. Sophie's friends were all nice, but there was a language barrier that kept me feeling like an outsider. I didn't overindulge and we left without much conversation to look back on.

Shopping

Like any Western travellers, we took part in the consumerist tradition of shopping, and found ourselves in a shopping centre many stories tall, full to the brim with knock-off brands. I was in awe at the likeness to the big brands that I knew from home. I stood at a makeup vendor with names like MAC, and saw eyeshadow palettes I recognized because they resembled famous ones. I saw headphones similar to Beats, at a fraction of the cost. I examined shoes in a wide assortment of colours, each with images of leaping pumas on the side, so similar to brands I was familiar with I wondered who could tell the difference.

I wanted a keepsake, but I didn't want to spend too much money. I ended up buying a very affordable little brown coin purse with a funny saying printed on the front of it in both Mandarin and clunky English: "money for fun time," or something like that.

Karaoke

Sophie explained that karaoke was a big thing in China. It was very different from what we knew karaoke to be in Canada, mostly consisting of drunk people finding the courage that others wished they didn't have, belting songs out at the top of their lungs in a sloppy manner that was forgotten about by the next morning. In Shanghai, it was a much classier experience, where attendees rented a room for the evening and dressed up. It would be a foreign experience, in every sense of the term.

The three of us put on some nice clothes — though I was certainly underdressed — and met up with Sophie's local friends. We were led down dark hallways to a room with two rows of benches on one end and an overhead projector illuminating the opposite wall. The projector displayed song titles, which we were able to select from, and the lyrics to sing along. There were also two microphones at the front of the room, ready and waiting for hot mouths to be pressed against them.

I've always enjoyed singing in the car, but I would never fool myself into thinking that I have an ounce of talent in the vocal department. I don't know how, but every other person in our karaoke room was Adele-in-the-making. They had voices of angels, which I noticed even before we put in mass orders for green tea whiskey. Anna and I mustered up some false courage and sang a couple of songs after consuming ungodly amounts of that green tea whiskey (which I had never had before, but can now vouch is quite dangerous). As the night progressed, I started chatting with this nice Chinese boy named Henry. We went out into the hall to hear one another better and ended up innocently kissing.

Sophie informed Anna and I that we were now moving the party elsewhere; I think our room rental was expiring. At this point, the green tea whiskey had really set in, and my memories of the evening get a bit foggy. I know that we ended up at a late-night club, and that when we entered I handed my coat to the coat check people. In a last-minute whiskey-hazed (horrible) decision, I decided that I didn't want to carry around my bulky purse all night. I handed it to the woman at the coat check along with my coat.

Henry and I left the club shortly after, through a side door so that we could sit outside in the fresh air. We continued to chat for a while, then finally re-entered the club in search of Anna and Sophie. They were nowhere to be seen. That's when I realized that I was in a foreign country where almost everyone around me spoke a different language. When I went to the coat check and found my jacket but no purse, I sobered up.

The Next Morning

Luckily for me, Henry was a great guy and contacted all of his friends who had been there that night in search of Sophie's address. I was able to crash at his place after a truly exhausting night. In the morning, he wrote an address down in Mandarin on a scrap piece of paper and handed it to me, instructing me to show it to a cab driver. I was hung over and hurting, and trying to ignore the sensory overload when I stepped outside into the bright, bustling, and booming streets.

As I hailed a taxi, I realized that this was the only way I could find my friends. My grip on the paper tightened. I could not believe my idiocy the night before, handing off my purse in such a nonchalant manner. Thank God, I thought, I'd removed my passport at Sophie's earlier that day, along with my driver's license. The only things of value that I lost were my debit card and a small amount of cash.

When I stumbled into Sophie's apartment, rather than being completely elated to see me (which is what I'd been anticipating), she asked if Anna was with me. Apparently, both of us had gone missing overnight.

Pollution

Anna returned to the apartment within an hour or so of me. We hung out on the couch in a hungover mess for the majority of the day. I showered, blowing my nose after patting myself dry.

"I blew my nose and the Kleenex was, like, grey," I said to Anna and Sophie, trying to hide the mix of disgust and concern in my voice.

"When I first moved here," Sophie began, "my chest started hurting. So after a few months, I went to the doctor to find out what was wrong with me. It was like my lungs were sore. The doctor listened to them and asked how long I'd been in China. I told him just a few months. He said that my body was just adjusting to the air quality here," she explained.

"Now I look online to see the air quality rating each day, and when it's really poor I wear a mask. I don't want to live here for too many years because I'm genuinely concerned about what it'll do to my health long-term," she admitted. "But that's what it was, pollution when you blew your nose."

Body Betrayal

For our final evening, we left Sophie's apartment for a nice dinner out. I was feeling incredibly unwell at this point, and was unable to pin it on one root cause. I knew that I was anxious regarding my lost belongings, and had incurred lasting effects from my alcohol abuse the night prior. We ordered several platters of dumplings, and I left momentarily to relieve myself in the washroom. While there, I discovered I had also begun my period, which explained some of my cramping. Sadly, I was unable to eat much of the meal and was still expected to pay for my third. When you're abroad and want to experience the cultural cuisine, there really is nothing more disappointing than your own body betraying you.

Onward

Sophie had to get to work the next morning, so we decided to pack up and head out so that she could lock up behind us. Anna and I hauled our suitcases behind us as we left the comfort of Sophie's apartment and entered the bustle of the Shanghai streets for the final time. We said our goodbyes to Sophie and jumped into a cab to the airport. We were willing to be early rather than to have some mishap or misfortune and miss our flight to Hong Kong.

This was our final drive on the tumultuous highways in China, an experience that I fear I will never forget. We paid our fare and headed into the airport on still-shaking legs.

As we approached the desk to check in, we were notified that we were far too early and would have to wait until an appropriate time closer to our departure. The airport itself was empty, so this was shocking news. We sat and got a coffee at one of the outrageously overpriced airport cafes; you know they just wait for suckers like us who will pay five times the going rate for a hot beverage to sip on while waiting patiently for the minutes to tick by.

Finally, we were allowed to check in, and we handed over our luggage. I was happy to be rid of it, thinking how much lighter I'd feel without towing it behind me. Only moments later I was directed into a room behind the scenes where I was asked if the black suitcase splayed open was mine. I said yes, wondering why in the hell all of my things were open and why my laptop was sitting out. I never got an answer to this question. The airport security nodded and continued on as if nothing of consequence had just occurred, and informed me I was free to leave to await the boarding call.

Hong Kong

We landed in Hong Kong in the evening, but I could still make out that we were surrounded by palm trees. I knew immediately how different it was from the crowded streets of Shanghai.

We were greeted by Lily, another one of Anna's university friends. I'd met her before, but unlike with Sophie, felt a bit guarded around her. She was nice, but had a colder demeanor than Sophie and kept me at a distance. I found her harder to read, which in turn made it more difficult for me to open up. It's interesting that I ended up stripping, exposing myself in so many ways. What most people don't realize is that you can stand in front of others fully naked and still have your guard up. Vulnerability is tricky like that.

The next day, Anna and I explored while Lily worked.

Hong Kong consisted of high-rise buildings in the midst of a tropical paradise. Walking around the downtown district we were surrounded by luxury brand names in large letters — no knock-offs here. It was a strange reminder that status and money are an inescapable part of the human experience.

Palm Reader

One evening after Lily got home from work, we ventured out to a night market and walked around. We came upon a booth with an older man who claimed to be a palm reader. I'd always been interested in any type of fortune-telling: suspicious of people who claim to have abilities, yet hopeful that someone could provide me with answers.

Anna went first. She placed both of her hands on top of his, palms facing up. The man seemed wise and sure of himself. He spoke English, but didn't have the vocabulary to describe in detail what he wanted to say. Our friend helped translate for us. Anna was apparently "competitive and stubborn, to the point where she would lose relationships with friends and family when they disagreed with her." She was also told that she was "incredibly driven, which could make her very successful in any career that she felt passion for."

When it was my turn, he gently took my hands and examined them. My reading couldn't have been further from Anna's. Where her focus was on her career and drive, mine was on my relationships. He told me that I would be content in my career, but that it wouldn't be the primary focus of my life. He said that my family mattered a lot to me (which was and is definitely true). The main source of pain in my life would stem from my intimate relationships. Lots of people would "have crushes on me," he said, and I'd have a lot of "loose ends." Sadly, I can confirm that this would also come true. I have been fortunate enough to have many intimate relationships over the years, but they always ended for reasons unrelated to incompatibility. The timing was always wrong. One of us was always moving. Still, we almost always ended on good terms. The palm reader said that I would need to "just pick someone and decide to stay with them." How romantic, I thought to myself.

The Land Down Under

Anna and I had of course tried to buy the cheapest flights possible, since money was tight. We each had some funds in our bank accounts, but we also needed to start paying back our student loans. The money we did have wasn't truly ours. As a result, we had an insanely long layover in the Kuala Lumpur airport while travelling to Australia. We were beyond exhausted, unable to keep our heads up or our eyes open. We began wandering the airport aimlessly, feeling foggy and intoxicated.

At some point, we came across those leather lounge chairs that you can sit in and pay for a massage. We rested there until airport security asked us to leave if we weren't paying. So we kept wandering until we found a few dozen other people like ourselves, curled up on a carpeted area under a walkway with security guards watching over them. Anna and I looked at each other and silently agreed that this was where we would rest our heavy heads. As I curled my body into a ball, much like a cat taking an afternoon nap, I placed my head on my purse and glanced around. I felt disgusting laying on that dirty carpet.

Hours — or was it only minutes? — later, there was an announcement on the loudspeaker, and the guards asked us to please get up and continue on with our day.

We landed in Melbourne, and I met Anna's aunt, Camille, and her husband, Ken. Camille was a tiny woman who spoke with a mixed Australian and French accent. She was all smiles, and incredibly welcoming. The yin to her yang, Ken, was a large man with a deep voice and a solemn face. I decided immediately: I liked them.

It was late when our plane landed, so we couldn't see much out the windows as we drove to their house in the suburbs. We were given a bedroom to share, and we quickly crawled into bed, relieved to have finally reached our destination. Laying in those clean sheets, it felt like a cloud had enveloped me in a warm embrace.

The next morning I awoke to see that the house itself was full of natural light, with windows everywhere. The room Anna and I were staying in was small, with a large wooden trunk for us to place some belongings in. The bed was a double bed; luckily we were close, so the lack of space wasn't an issue. The floors throughout the home were wood, and the kitchen was open to the dining room on one side, where you could walk down a few steps into the living room and find a TV and comfy couches. It immediately felt like home.

Settling In

Over the next few weeks, Anna and I would wake up each morning without the help of an alarm clock, make ourselves a nice breakfast, and sit down to enjoy a cup of coffee. Waking up with the sun shining through the windows, and with the seemingly new realization that we were in Australia, never failed to put me in a chipper mood. Without anything on the agenda, we had no stress or worries. We enjoyed looking at the brightly coloured cockatoos just outside the house, sitting on the branches of trees.

Camille and Ken welcomed us into the area. They took us to a local wildlife sanctuary, where we spent the day walking around in the sunshine and heat, getting to see all of the critters that we'd only ever seen pictures of. The furry koalas slept soundly in the trees, and the dingos paced around their enclosures.

Anna and I walked all over the suburb to different shops and restaurants, where we occasionally went out for brunches and dinners. Around this time, we started discussing our financial situation. We knew that we didn't have the expenses of rent and groceries at tha moment, but we were also acutely aware that we'd be running out of money sooner rather than later. It wasn't that we were spending a lot, it was more the fact that neither of us had much saved before leaving home. We'd originally planned to search for jobs and an apartment once we'd arrived in Australia, and decided that we needed to start doing that. We appreciated the generosity shown by Camille and Ken, and felt comfortable in their home, but we also didn't want to overstay our welcome. It felt like visiting family. Instead, we wanted to experience life in Melbourne as twenty-three--year-olds: meeting other young people, going out, drinking, and exploring the sights.

We began looking for apartments online, hunting for a place to rent downtown. We were shocked when we saw the prices. Everything was insanely expensive. And unlike in Canada, rent wasn't priced out on a monthly basis but rather a weekly basis, so it was all very deceiving. *This is going to be much more difficult than we'd originally anticipated,* I thought to myself.

Employment

We booked a few apartment viewings in the downtown core of Melbourne. We desperately wanted a central location, where we could walk to stores and restaurants rather than rely on public transportation as we'd been doing. The suburbs we were staying in were a decent drive from the city as it was, but taking the bus was a chore. It involved numerous routes, and even when timed perfectly (which was often not the case), it took well over an hour. Realistically, the one-way trek took us at least an hour and a half.

The apartments we saw were great, but when we showed any serious interest, the real estate agents handed us a lengthy application to fill out. It looked like a job application, and asked us for details such as current employer and references. This was completely unlike anything I'd seen back in Canada. Apparently they could ask for these details because it was so competitive to find a place. It felt a bit invasive, but the even more glaring issue was that neither of us even had an income.

Anna and I realized that in order to get our own space, we might have to look at acquiring some sort of employment first. Anna was interested in serving or bartending. She'd worked at restaurants in Canada previously, so her experience should get her in the door, she explained to me.

I countered, suggesting we look into stripping. Yes, I was the one who had the idea and voiced it to Anna. I'm sure anyone who knows us would be shocked to hear this, since she was the one in high school who didn't give a shit what others thought, while I was the quiet "booksmart" girl. She was the ballsy one of the two of us. She was the one who went to McGill University to escape Ontario and start drinking and clubbing at eighteen instead of waiting until nineteen like the rest of us. She was the one who had her eyebrow pierced in high school, which looked absolutely badass (although she managed to pull it off in a feminine, hippy-esque way rather than the hard way I'm sure you initially imagined). She's always been much shorter than me, a ball of energy and self-confidence. So after my out-of-character suggestion, she quickly agreed that we should look into exotic dancing. She was just as interested in the taboo nightlife as I was. And what better place to try something new that could easily tarnish your reputation than on the other side of the world?

The first thing we did was sit on the bed in the guest room we were staying in at Camille's. I opened up my laptop and searched local strip clubs. We came across one located right downtown, which seemed promising and had a page designated to employment opportunities, with a spot that gave information to contact them.

We were already planning to visit the city one evening that week with Camille and Ken, who were going to a concert. They'd invited us to tag along for the drive, so that we could explore while they enjoyed their show. Of course, we'd seen how long the ride was via bus, so we'd happily agreed.

When we got to Melbourne that night, we told them we'd wander around and might get a bite to eat. We said our goodbyes, and then Anna and I hopped on a streetcar and headed to the location of the club.

The only time I'd ever stepped foot inside a strip club was with two of my roommates about a year prior. We'd done a combined birthday celebration for two of us who were born around the same time. The three of us visited a male strip club that night. The drinks were insanely overpriced, resulting in me ordering just one sugary cocktail ;thankfully we had already consumed a number of sangrias with dinner. I remembered noticing the strange layout of the place. It was narrow and long, which meant you were either seated at the stage or in back. We tried to sit in the back ourselves and learned it was reserved for bachelorette parties. The dancers were either adorable — puppy dog cute — or super creepy and exhibitionist, nearly jacking off on stage. It was far from the best night of my life. Since then, I'd always based my thoughts on strip clubs off of that one experience. Thinking of it now, it's strange that I wanted to pursue dancing myself.

We recognized the place by the brightly lit sign outside, with additional light bulbs surrounding it in case anyone missed it. There was a bouncer dressed in black standing out front and a velvet rope strung across golden barriers, I assume to direct a line when it got busier. It wasn't needed when we arrived, since there was no one else waiting to be let in. Anna and I looked at one another for reassurance, and handed the bouncer our IDs for entrance.

We walked in, not sure what to expect, and walked down a dark set of stairs into a dimly lit area. The whole room was dark, with black marble floors and grey stools with gold legs. Directly in the center of the room — the only area that had proper lighting — was a small stage with a single pole in the middle. There were shorter stools all around the stage for those who wanted an intimate view. We saw a very petite woman on stage with a one-piece black outfit, dark hair, and red lips. There were a few customers in the crowd, but overall the club was quite empty.

"Drink?" we asked one another simultaneously. Something we've never disagreed on is our instinct to rely on alcohol when faced with a socially awkward situation. Anna and I hurried to the bar and each ordered a beer. The bar was backlit with a blue LED light, giving off a cool glow.

"Let's take a seat somewhere, but not too close to the stage?" I said in a question rather than a statement, wanting to see if Anna agreed with me.

"Why not up front?" she demanded.

"Well... it's not very busy, and I don't want to draw attention to us. Plus, I don't know if you're going to, but I don't have money to tip them, and I feel like that's kinda expected at the stage..."

"Yeah, you're right,." She nodded in agreement. "We're basically here to gain intel."

The dancers wandered around in bras and underwear, high stripper heels, and little dresses or skirts. Some were mingling with patrons, but many were just sitting with a drink in hand, talking to one another. As one particularly stunning girl walked past, Anna turned to me.

"Okay, I'll try to get her attention." She turned back and started speaking to the dancer. I could barely hear what she said over the music, but the dancer nodded her head and stopped beside Anna, listening. I moved closer to join the conversation.

"This is my friend," Anna said, gesturing to me. I smiled and gave a small wave. "We're interested in getting jobs here."

The dancer had long dark hair and a naturally gorgeous face. "Yeah, no problem. I'm Mikayla. What questions do you have? I haven't worked here for that long."

After some lighter conversation, Anna got straight to the point. "What kind of money do you make, if you don't mind me asking?"

We found out that Mikayla was from another city, and was travelling around Australia with her boyfriend. She made enough money after three nights of work to live off of with her boyfriend for a week or two. Then she'd work again when she needed to.

We thanked Mikayla for her time and openness talking with us, finished our beers, and looked for the exit. After checking the time, we discovered we were running behind schedule. After Camille and Ken had shown us so much generosity, the last thing we wanted to do was make them wait. We ran to the streetcar and leaped on, only to find out we were going the wrong way. Soon, we found ourselves sprinting down the streets of Melbourne as fast as we possibly could in our flip flops and short shorts. I'm sure we were quite the sight.

We made it back to the car and explained that we'd lost track of time at dinner, then headed back home with our hosts, feeling no guilt for the little white lie.

Audition

Anna and I decided we'd take the next step towards working at this club. The girl we'd spoken with, Mikayla, made it sound appealing, especially for us in our less-than-impressive financial situation. We liked the idea of having freedom during the day to explore and sightsee, leaving our evenings for work. We wanted to meet other young travellers and explore the continent, just like Mikayla said she did with her boyfriend.

I'd be lying if I said that there wasn't a small part of me that was excited to experience life as a stripper. I wanted to see what it would be like to feel sexy all the time, and to be surrounded by other women doing the same thing. I'd often been the object of desire at times when I didn't want the attention. Grocery shopping, hanging out with friends, taking my dog for a walk… Well, I thought, if it's going to happen anyways, why not try to profit off it? It's like the saying "if you can't beat 'em, join 'em"; if you can't strip yourself of your sex appeal entirely, you might as well strip your clothes and try to strip their money from them.

So we reached out to the managers asking for employment. One of them responded saying he'd be happy to meet with us and asked us to be there Friday night at 8 p.m. We happily agreed and made our way downtown.

Anna and I wandered into a bottle shop — or liquor store, as we call them in Canada — and got some very affordable wine. We walked the streets until we found a public washroom, and took turns chugging said wine until we could feel a buzz. Classy, I know. But we were hoping to start our careers in sex work, so it seemed like an appropriate way to begin.

The downtown area of Melbourne is grid-like, making it easy to maneuver without getting too lost or disoriented. We ventured down a side street from the main road where the club was located, and discovered some trendy restaurants. Anna and I found one that served drinks, and each ordered a beverage to supplement the wine we'd already had. We sat outside at a little round table with an umbrella overhead, feeling the cobblestone beneath our feet and the bustle of the city around us. The world felt loud, and I wasn't sure how much of it was around me and how much was in my own head. It was a weird feeling, being drawn into the darkness by promising whispers, but also being fully aware that when Alice took that single step into the rabbit hole, she lost all control.

It was time. We got up and walked back to the club, entering that staircase again and walking down into the dark. Anna and I were greeted by a middle-aged, toad-like man named Todd. He led us to an elevator in the corner of the club. We followed him in, and went down a level to the basement. Todd took us to a small room and sat behind a large desk, and we mirrored him, sitting in chairs across from him. It felt like we were in a principal's office in preparation for a scolding. I'd imagine, anyway; I'd never gotten into any trouble throughout my schooling years.

Todd asked us if we'd danced before, and we told him openly that we hadn't. We were interested in dancing and had spoken to one of the girls there, who said she liked it and made good money. We explained that we were from Canada, and had Working Holiday Visas.

He then calmly asked us to show him what we were working with. Anna looked at me with fear in her eyes.

"Please take off your clothes," Todd clarified. Neither of us moved. "Well how do you expect to do it for hundreds of people in a night here if you can't even do it for me?" He had a point. We both stood up and took off our clothes, leaving our bras and thongs on. "Turn around," he instructed without much expression on his face. We did, and then quickly dressed again.

"You can start tomorrow night," he stated. He had us fill out forms with our information and photocopied our IDs.

Todd explained that we would pay him and his co-manager, Steve, a certain amount to work for the night. After that, any extra money we made was ours to keep. This was standard in Melbourne. Essentially, strippers were independent contractors, which meant you worked for yourself but paid the club for the ability to work there. At this particular club, we owed Todd and Steve $65 if we started work at 7:30 p.m., right when they opened. For every hour later that we showed up, we owed them more money. As a result, Anna and I would show up at 7:30 p.m. almost every night we worked there.

Alter Ego

"I think I'm gonna be Amber," I said confidently to Anna. We were lying on the bed in our room at Camille and Ken's place, wasting time on laptops in the afternoon heat.

"Why Amber?"

"Well, Amber Rose was a stripper, so it just fits. Plus, I just like the name." I especially liked the femininity of the name, since my parents had blessed me with a boy's name.

"I'm gonna go by Mickey," Amber decided.

And thus, we were reborn. It's weird picking out your own name, and even weirder introducing yourself by this name to nearly everyone you meet going forward. A name to hide behind, a persona to create. Time would prove that I absolutely suck at being disingenuous, but at that moment, I couldn't wait to meet Amber.

Costume

Todd had told us what sort of attire was required to work at the club. We needed to get heels, of course, but we also needed lingerie and some sort of skirt or dress to wear over top, which we were to take off at the end of the first song on stage. We'd spent a bit of time watching the performers when we went for our "audition," or job interview — whatever you'd call the experience of a middle-aged man asking to see us in our underwear.

We noticed that the girls all wore different things: some wore short skirts, others transparent yet elegant nightgowns over top of their underwear and bras. Some of them wore full-bottomed underwear, but the majority wore thongs. Everyone wore outrageously high heels, but some of the shoes were clear plastic while others were neon colours. Some girls wore black studded heels, and some were slip-ons with only one strap on top of the foot, while others clasped closed.

On our first day, Anna and I went into the downtown core a few hours early with the hopes of finding outfits. We brought some extra makeup along, since we were just wearing minimal everyday looks for our shopping trip. We went into a large department store and found the lingerie section, perusing and eventually picking out some cute things to try on. It felt like we were deceiving the older store clerks, as we appeared to be picking out lingerie for the eyes of our partners in private bedrooms, not for the eyes of whatever strangers happened to come into the club. A small part of me felt gross about it, but I mostly just felt like we had a mission, and we were there to complete it.

I ended up purchasing a black lace bra and underwear set with light pink detailing. It was cute but minimal, and the bra didn't have any push-up or anything. The bottoms were what you'd describe as "cheeky," which to girls with small bottoms means full coverage, but to me meant it rides up your ass and everything's out for display. Which was fine, because that's the whole point, right?

Anna purchased a few things as well, and we were onto our next item on the list: stripper heels. She looked at me quizzically. "Where would you get something like that? Do you think we have to go to a sex shop?"

"I honestly have no idea," I replied with a shrug. Neither of us had the slightest clue where to go to buy these types of shoes; I couldn't remember ever seeing them at stores in the past. So the hunt was on. We left the department store and headed back onto one of the main streets downtown, wandering in a random direction and glancing in each shop window as we passed.

"Let's go in here, it looks like they have a wide variety of shoes," Anna said, pointing to a storefront. As soon as we opened the door, I saw what she meant. The store carried an extensive, eclectic mix of shoes. There were strappy silver and gold sandals, Gladiator-style, and sneakers with what looked like bright splotches of paint covering them. Some were what I'd describe as "emo" or punk rock, black knee-high platform boots with silver studs.

"Look!" Anna stole my attention from the boots I'd imagined KISS might wear onstage. She was holding up a white pair of stripper heels. I made my way over to her, and saw that there were several pairs to choose from. I picked out a black pair with some small rhinestones on them. They had a clasp, and good thing, because I was intimidated by their height and didn't want to risk falling out of them. The brand was called Pleaser, and the heel was seven inches (which I'd soon come to learn wasn't even considered that high for dancers). Anna's white pair clasped as well. We paid, and unlike my experience purchasing my lingerie, I didn't feel like a liar at all. I would, in fact, be wearing these shoes in a matter of hours for my first night stripping. I didn't feel like I was trying to conceal anything.

The First Dance

The dancers entered the club from a side entrance, which was placed indiscreetly right around the corner from the main entrance. Any idiot onlooker could see that you worked there and were going inside to strip. I didn't mind, but I still don't understand why they designed the place this way, as if entering a separate door made a difference.

Anna and I pressed the buzzer, and the security guard asked who it was. "Amber and Mickey," Anna answered into the speaker. There was a camera above us as well.

"Okay, c'mon in."

We opened the heavy door and walked downstairs into the basement changeroom. The room was long and narrow, with shelves on one side and a wall of mirrors on the other. There were already several hair straighteners plugged in and heating up on the countertop where the mirrors were, preparing for the night.

I opened my bag and removed my new black lingerie, as well as a skirt I'd packed from my own suitcase. It was a simple black skirt that was tight around the waist and flared out, hitting my upper thighs. It made me look thinner since it showed off my smaller waist and glided over my curviest parts.

I strapped on my heels, looked at my reflection in the mirror, and applied some lip gloss for good measure. Anna was doing up her own heels. She stood up straight, and we looked at one another, taking deep breaths.

Todd walked into the changeroom and introduced us to a girl with black hair. "This is Zena. She'll show you guys the ropes tonight. Any questions, ask her." He left the room just as quickly as he'd arrived.

"Hi, it's nice to meet you. I'm Mickey," Anna said.

"I'm Amber," I followed suit.

"Have either of you danced before?" she asked candidly.

We shook our heads in unison, probably looking moronic and naive.

"That's fine, just ask me if you have any questions." She turned and bounced out of the room. That was a short introduction, I thought to myself.

"Well, I guess this is it," I said, just as much to myself as to Anna.

"Okay, do we have everything we need? We have our wallets, I guess we're good to go."

We walked like baby gazelles teetering precariously in our heels over to the elevator. We stepped inside and pressed the button to go up into the club. The music was blasting as my eyes adjusted to the darkness, and I scanned the room to see how many customers there were. Not many... Which was probably a good thing, I determined. Fewer people to embarrass myself in front of.

Zena was already on the main stage, and clearly was not lacking in confidence. She moved like she was sure of herself. It wasn't quite sexy, but it was skillful, and it looked like she was enjoying the music.

Anna and I sat down off to the side, watching Zena.

"Wow, she's awesome. She really knows what she's doing," Anna said. She was in awe.

"Yeah... I'm so scared to go up there alone." Both of my hands clasped around my wallet nervously. I had no idea what I was doing. Todd had explained that we'd go on stage when the announcer — who spoke into the microphone, amping up each girl to the audience — called our names. We had to stay on the main stage for two songs, and needed to have our tops off by the end of the first one. We were instructed to keep our underwear on for the whole thing, unless someone tipped us. In that case, we were expected to remove our panties. For whatever reason, that felt too revealing to me. Being almost completely naked on stage was fine, but the thin piece of fabric covering my genitals was the only thing holding my morals intact at this point. After the main stage, we were to make our way immediately to the smaller side stage, which resembled a podium, to do another two songs. In case anyone wanted a private dance, there were two smaller rooms off the sides of the club with benches all around them. It was $50 for two songs there. Hidden in the very back corner — which we didn't even see when we first came to inspect the club — a third private dance room was tucked away. This area was delegated for VIP dances only, meaning that it was reserved for when customers wanted to buy a longer time period with you. This could be one hour, or four. This was a lot more money, and quite rare, by the sounds of it, since Todd didn't bother spending time explaining prices with us.

"Next up, Amba!" the announcer exclaimed into the microphone. I guess I hadn't fully thought the name through, not realizing that an Aussie accent wouldn't pronounce the "r" sound. I made my way behind the stage and sat in the wings until Zena finished her second song.

The music ended and she ran off, clutching cash in her hands. The song started, and my heart pumped along to the bass, adrenaline shooting through my body. I made my way out into the spotlight and began moving to the music. It was kind of surreal. It was at that moment that I realized how much I enjoy attention. I think I've always just had a desire to be wanted. It showed in my dancing, as the main goal was to entice onlookers. To want to be wanted. It felt kind of great to have all eyes on me while I swayed back and forth to the music. I unzipped the black skirt and stepped out of it, tossing it to the back of the stage. I went out and moved around the pole, not daring to try any tricks as I was sure I'd humiliate myself. The first song ended and I remembered the rules — I had to take my top off. I did, and felt like I was shedding my skin, a past part of me that no longer fit, no longer benefitted me.

I continued to move until the second song ended, running off and ensuring I grabbed my bra and skirt on the way.

As I made my way to the podium stage, buckling my bra as I went, I realized that I could do this. I finished my set while glancing at the crowd and at Anna — Mickey — who was now on the main stage doing her thing. Her small ankles looked dangerously close to snapping in her heels. She had much more experience with professional dance than I did, doing everything from ballet to tap for most of her life. I did hip-hop with her throughout high school, but wasn't as technically knowledgeable. What I learned was that in the strip club, none of that matters. Anna moved in a much different way than I did, but no better or worse.

I finished my set and realized that dancing for four songs straight in seven-inch heels was quite the workout. I took a seat at a bench on the side of the club, and eventually Anna joined me.

"So, how did you find it?" she asked excitedly.

"It was terrifying, but then not nearly as bad as I expected! I mean, I'm sure it'll be different when it's really busy, but once I was on stage and started dancing I felt fine," I said.

"Yeah, it wasn't bad!"

An old man who was clearly inebriated approached me and asked for a dance. I felt my stomach drop as I replied that I could definitely dance for him. I stood up and led him to one of the private rooms. He took a seat, and I asked for the $50 cash. Then I began moving over top of him, removing my bra and shifting from facing him to facing away from him. He reached for my breasts, and I grabbed his hands, pinning them over his head. He grumbled something about touching, and I replied, "That's not allowed," as matter-of-factly as I could.

When the dance ended, he got up furiously, stating that it was the worst dance he's ever had. I didn't care — my first dance was done! Thrilled and confused, I left the room and sat down with Anna. I glanced into the room where Zena was and saw that the gentleman she was dancing for was, in fact, touching her stomach and boobs. Oh, shit. I don't know why I was so sure that they weren't supposed to touch.

The night continued and I ended up doing a few more dances, this time actually allowing the men to touch my chest and stomach. Apparently, the line was drawn at the genitals. They couldn't grope my vagina, but tits was fine.

I was relieved to be done with my first shift, with some cash in my wallet to show for it. I was feeling a bit ashamed at how my initial dance had gone, but it wasn't something I felt like sharing with anyone, so I kept my thoughts and feelings to myself.

Zena checked in with us, asking us how our night had gone, and the three of us took the elevator back to the changeroom. Anna and I removed our heels, which was honestly better than an orgasm. We put our clothes over top of our lingerie and slipped into our flip flops, disoriented at where the exit was after that long shift.

Lighting (or Lack Thereof)

I've since spoken to some friends who have asked me, "Weren't you insecure that everyone could see your flaws? Your cellulite, or hair that you might have missed shaving?" The first thing I tell these friends is that, with a naked woman in front of them, most people are in awe and not looking at the little things. Besides that, anyone who's ever been inside a strip club knows they are notorious for being dimly lit. While this gives off a cool vibe, it also greatly benefits the dancers. It works to hide all these little details that we might nitpick about ourselves. In this nightlife, cellulite, scars, ingrown hairs, and spider veins don't exist!

Devon

It turned out that the skinny girl we'd seen onstage when we first visited the club was from Canada too. She was from Quebec, and went by the name Devon. I had no desire to get to know her, mainly because she seemed cold. I'd also seen the way she interacted with others, and something about it irritated me. She was constantly sticking out her ass and fake laughing far too loudly. She just rubbed me the wrong way.

Devon had befriended another dancer, who went by Sophia. Their friendship didn't make sense to me. Sophia was quiet and had a tenderness about her. She was short and curvy, with a gorgeous old-Hollywood beauty, sharp cheekbones and cat-eye makeup. It wasn't until months later when I saw a poster of Sophia Loren that I thought to myself, Wow, Sophia Loren looks exactly like Sophia from the club. I felt like a fool as I realized she probably did her makeup to emulate the actress, emphasizing their natural resemblance.

One night, Devon was speaking openly about how she'd gone to the casino with the money she'd made the night before, and put it all on red. She'd won, doubling her money. Apparently, she'd also sold a few baggies of coke in the VIP room while giving dances. I hadn't been aware that this sort of thing was going down at the club, but I wasn't surprised. I'm not an idiot. I just didn't know who was partaking in these activities until that moment.

Anna and I ventured over to the casino ourselves sometimes after late nights working. We even played roulette, though we played $20 at a time instead of the $600 Devon claimed to have bet. One night I was on a winning streak, eventually walking out with a few extra hundred dollars I'd collected after winning a number of smaller bets. Unfortunately, I returned to the casino a few weeks later thinking it would happen again, and I lost all the money I'd made. I hadn't thought my luck would run out.

Little White Lies

"I'm supposed to be Skyping with my parents tonight," I explained to Anna one day. "I can't lie. I just cannot lie. My family knows me too well."

"Why can't you just tell them we're serving? Here, I'll find out more info about the casino downtown, and we'll say we've been working there, serving and wiping up tables. It's pretty believable with our weird hours." I'd seen Anna tell white lies before. She was the opposite of me: cool, calm, collected and most importantly, entirely believable.

She would research first to build her story and provide enough details that no one would question her, but not enough to lead you to think she was overcompensating. This was a skill I didn't have much use for before this job, and one that I hadn't really practiced.

"Here's the website. Let's look at the photos so we can describe it a bit," she suggests, pointing to the screen. "This is perfect, because we need to tell Camille something too. She's so nice letting us stay here, and I feel bad about lying." She bites her lower lip, but her voice doesn't reveal any feelings of remorse. "We need a story that makes sense for our late nights."

I'd been dodging a real conversation with my parents since losing my phone in Shanghai, and my mom had asked why I wasn't answering on WhatsApp. I'd brushed it off because I didn't want to seem irresponsible, losing my phone at our first destination. Instead, I'd communicated through Facebook Messenger, saying that I wasn't online much and was busy exploring and searching for work.

The evening came, and I finally Skyped with my parents. When they asked me about work, I paused, and then restated some of the things Anna had said earlier. We'd been fortunate to get work at a bar in the casino in Melbourne, and were mainly serving customers and wiping down tables. The hours sucked since it was late at night, but the pay was alright since their minimum wage was so much better than Canada, and we got some tips on top of that. I then pretended the Internet connection was bad, and logged off. It felt like such a shameful thing to do, but there you have it. I was the cowardly lion from the Wizard of Oz, hiding behind my computer screen, unable to own up to my own shit.

Zipper Down

During an uneventful shift, I was speaking with a gentleman with a strong accent. He was communicating fine, but it was obvious that English wasn't his first language. He'd asked for a dance, so I led the way to one of the private rooms. As he was sitting down, I saw his hand swiftly move downwards. In a terrible flash, he managed to unzip his pants and grab at his flaccid penis, exposing it.

In horror, I clarified as quickly as I could, "Oh no, no, you can't do that! Please put it away! Put it away!"

He placed his penis back into his pants, zipped them up, and looked innocently at my face, which I'm certain revealed my true emotions.

The really messed up thing about this encounter was how ashamed I was left feeling, thinking perhaps I'd managed to miscommunicate somewhere along the line.

With Friends Like These...

Todd and Steve had let us know that all the new girls had to work "poker night" at the club. Poker night was held on Tuesday nights, and we learned pretty quickly that the mandatory shift for new girls was because no one came. They needed dancers to work, but the poker players who showed up were there to play poker, not to buy dances. So we played, too.

It was a night like this where I met Louis. He was fairly young, probably in his early thirties, and had a kind smile. Louis always came with his friend Rob, another young guy. They bought drinks and invited me to sit with them. It was nice to chat with young people and hear a bit about their lives, sharing a bit about my own in return. I learned that Louis was originally from Sri Lanka, where his parents still lived. He'd actually applied to immigrate to Canada and Australia, but happened to get accepted to Australia first.

I sat beside Louis for hours. He ordered me Cokes, always asking, "Would you like a Coke?" When I replied, "Yes, please," he was always sure to clarify, "Not the drug, I mean the drink." We both proceeded to chuckle, as if the joke never got old. I'd always assure him that no, I didn't do drugs anyway. He also called me "Cindy" instead of Amber, because he insisted that I looked like Cindy Crawford — which I vehemently disagreed with, but will forever be one of the best compliments I've ever received. I don't think anyone would mind being compared to a supermodel.

As we left the club, Anna interrogated me. "You probably did well tonight, sitting with Louis the whole time. How much did you make?"

"Um, I did alright."

"Why won't you tell me how much?"

Maybe it's how I was raised, but that's a rude question to ask. I didn't think stripping would be for us if we were comparing. Money or bodies, comparison is not the most beneficial thing for your mental health. Still, it's something that we do naturally. It's human nature to get a bit envious when you see another dancer getting hauled back to do private dances all night while you struggle to get any, or overhearing a dancer chatting with their friend in the changeroom at the end of the night about how they made a shit-ton of money. That doesn't mean it's what we should be doing.

"I don't think we should compare."

She went off, letting me know just how strongly she disagreed.

"That's my friend," I explained to Crystal, a kind Australian girl with long dirty blonde hair and fake boobs who sat across from me. It turns out that Anna had made some enemies in our club because she'd refused to leave a customer who had already been talking with another girl.

"There's stripper etiquette," Crystal countered. "It's just an unspoken rule, you don't do that."

"Yeah, I get that," I replied. "She got in trouble for dancing for less than $50 last night. She wanted the money so she bargained for $40. Zena told her straight up at the end of the night that she can't do that, because it fucks over the other dancers who are charging the proper amount." I wasn't overly surprised that she'd done this, since money clearly mattered to her, but I get why the other girls were pissed. There are set prices for a reason.

I told Crystal that Anna and I'd had some arguments since we'd left Canada, too, and I wasn't sure that being with each other all the time was a great idea.

"You should travel on your own. I'm saying this based on what I've seen from her and her vibes. She's selfish, and you need to do what's best for you." Crystal's concern for me seemed genuine, as she stared directly at me with her doll eyes.

Period

Ah, the joy of stripping on your menstrual cycle! The first time I had my period while dancing, I was nervous about leakage. Anna wore a menstrual cup, a wonderful invention that I would have loved to try, but due to my IUD — intrauterine device, a form of long-term birth control — my doctor had advised me not to use one. Apparently, the suction that it creates has the possibility of dislodging an IUD, which I certainly didn't want to risk. Instead, I found that most girls just used a tampon and cut the string short, shoving it as far inside as possible. This worked for me, and I was fortunate to never experience standing up after a private dance to see red stains.

Pizza Pizza

"If I order pizza, I wanna eat it!" A young guy was yelling this over and over again. I was walking over to the bar, where the bartenders kept ice waters for girls to drink throughout the evening. I grabbed one and turned around, only to hear him yell out again, "If I order pizza, I wanna eat it!" This time he added, "If I'm paying, I wanna fuck!" Despite his appalling state, so intoxicated that he swayed, drenched in his own sweat, his words were crystal clear. I couldn't contain my chuckle, and patted his back as I walked by as dismissively as I could.

This comment sticks with me today for several reasons. Brothels are, in fact, legal in Australia. I've had numerous conversations with strip club patrons where I was surprised to learn that they'd used the services provided at brothels. I don't say that in a judgemental way at all. I know that prostitution is the oldest profession to exist, and I'm deeply respectful of sex workers, seeing as I myself was a stripper. I was, however, surprised to hear from some men in their twenties that they'd gone to a brothel for a friend's birthday party and each chosen a girl to sleep with. I think seeing such a young, good-looking guy admit to this so unabashedly was refreshing in a way. He was honest. Though I guess it has to be said, he was honest to a stripper named Amber, and had we been on a date or anywhere else, he may not have told me this story.

I don't know why this pizza fellow felt the need to yell this comment so insistently, or why he had even chosen to come to a strip club rather than a brothel. It's not as though the sign out front advertised anything other than women getting naked in front of you for money. We made no promises that we couldn't keep.

Sex workers are not unlike any other employees. They offer a service, and people are willing to pay for that service. Some people want the simple physical aspect of it. Show them the bodies and they're happy. Others, I learned through my own experience, want the company. They want a friend, a caring ear. These individuals are often completely unaware of the fact that you're naked. Some men even pay for private dances just to ask that you sit rather than dance, keeping your clothes on. You might think this is the easiest money, and sometimes that's the case. But not always. Sometimes people tell you really heartbreaking stories, and you become more of a therapist than anything else. This can be much more draining than the patrons who just want to see you move your body. Groups of partiers come in wanting to get wasted. Couples come in looking to spice up their sex lives and find passion they may have lost somewhere along the way. Every patron is different, and yet they're all drawn to the same place.

You cannot look at someone and know what their stories are. I've learned that this holds true for the person walking into a club just as much as it does for the dancers on stage.

Alex

"You in the white, come here! My friend says you're his perfect woman, he'd marry you!" I look back and see three guys around my own age, sitting and having a drink. They were off to the side of the club and far back from the main stage. Where people sit says a lot about them and the night they're looking to have. I could tell right away that they were just here to hang out and enjoy their drinks.

I got up and made my way back to them, introducing myself and asking how their night was going.

"It's going well, mate, how's yours? Eh, what's that accent, are you 'Merican?" one of them asked me. He reminded me of someone I knew from my hometown, those guys I went to high school with who were confident and sure of themselves.

"Canadian, an easy mistake to make. I won't hold it against you," I replied, as though I hadn't answered similarly dozens of times before.

"This here's my mate, Alex," the leader of the group continued. "He pointed to you and said you're a goddess, his perfect woman." He grinned in greeting. "I'm Max, and this here's my cousin, Luke."

"Is that so?" I looked seductively at Alex, noting how adorable he was. Hey, I may have been stripping, but I still had eyes. I was not immune to his handsome face and charming smile. When he stood up later, I also saw that the dude was around 6'8", probably one of the tallest guys I've ever seen.

"Yeah, I did say that. It's true, too," he said, taking me aback with his sheepishness. Apparently his friend's cockiness hadn't rubbed off on him.

We spoke for a bit, and I decided he was unlike a lot of the guys I'd met in their early twenties. He was conventionally attractive, but didn't act like he knew it. That's rare in this world. When he asked me for my number, I willingly gave it — breaking the unspoken rules of stripping, but I figured I might as well have some fun. He knew I was travelling and staying in Melbourne for an indefinite amount of time, and that was alright. We began exchanging messages daily, getting to know one another's lives more intimately.

Beauty

I was sitting in one of the side rooms after finishing a private dance, $50 richer, when the man decided to share something with me. "When I first saw you on stage, you were awkward and nervous. Then when I got a dance with you, you moved way too fast. But now," he said as though complimenting me, "you're slower and sexy."

"Oh, wow. Thanks," I replied, not sure what exactly he was looking for. Quite a backhanded compliment.

"You're the most beautiful woman I've ever seen in my life," he continued.

That's the thing about dancing: you will hear the most compliments in your life, and the most debasing criticisms. I happened to get both from this particular gentleman this evening.

It's best not to take things to heart, remembering that these people don't really know you. They merely know the facade you're putting on, the face you're portraying. As humans, though, it's harder than we'd think to completely forget everything we've been told.

Battle Scars

Over the course of my stripping career, I incurred many bruises. They mainly marked up my legs, especially my knees. Some women are skilled on the pole, lifting themselves up and performing mesmerizing tricks. I hadn't learned many moves, so I got into groundwork. This choice was partially because I'm lazy, and when you're tired from dancing in heels all night, the floor, though hard and slippery, seems more appealing than continuing to dance upright. It was also because I'm well aware that my best asset is, well, my ass.

One night I was sufficiently drunk, walking from the changerooms towards the elevator to enter the club before my next set on stage. The carpeted floor was already a design that resembled a Pollock painting, with splashes everywhere. To make matters worse for any inebriated women in sky-high heels, it was uneven, with bumps and ramps in unexpected places. As I attempted to step into the elevator with far too much confidence, my legs completely betrayed me. My ankle twisted, and my knee turned in a way that knees are not meant to turn. I collapsed to the ground in agony. My right knee burned fiercely, but I ignored the pain and lifted myself up as quickly as I could, scared someone had witnessed my wipeout. I made my way to the bar for a quick drink before powering through my next stage performance.

I had torn my meniscus terribly, and would spend months after that night sleeping with a pillow under my knee to ease the pain. To this day, if I move the wrong way, I injure the same knee again.

Dancers are badass.

Photoshoot

My mentality towards nudity and privacy had shifted greatly over the course of my first month stripping. It's funny how quickly that happens when you're in a new environment — how quickly that becomes your norm. I'd been looking at odd jobs online when I came across an advertisement for female models to do a photoshoot. The ad stated that it was a one-time thing, with potential for more shoots if the photographer liked your work.

There were some images attached to the ad to give potential applicants an idea of the work. The women were clothed, albeit scantily clad in bras and booty shorts. What the hell? I figured. I'm getting fully naked for strangers on a nightly basis at this point. Some nights I make shit pay. At least I'd know that I would walk away with a good amount of money after this. The ad explained that the shoots typically lasted about an hour, and that the pay was $400.

"What do you think of this?" I turned my laptop so Anna could read the ad. "It's easy money," I continued, biting my lip with hesitation.

"Yeah, and in the middle of the day, so we could still go to work. Why not?" Anna nodded.

I sent in my application, complete with a few images of myself. Within a day I was set to go for the following week. The email gave me a contact name and number, and a location where I would be meeting the photographer.

Camille drove us to Brighton Beach, which took just over half an hour to reach. It was a lovely day. Sunshine poured through the car windows, the warmth reaching the deepest parts of me. It always felt good to participate in activities during the daytime. I was able to merrily neglect all thoughts of my vampire nightlife and pretend that I normally attended events like this, amongst the living.

As we drove, I noted for the hundredth time how many of the vehicles were older than even myself. This was something that we rarely saw in Canada, with the four seasons wreaking havoc on vehicles until they were hazardous to navigate in. Here, vehicles sparkled in the sun as if they were almost brand new, their age given away just by their styles, which I'd only ever seen on TV.

When we parked and exited the car, I saw tanned young bodies, their long locks lightened from so much time spent outside. People were carrying their surfboards as they ran across the street barefoot. This was how I'd envisioned Australia before coming. Not spending my nights getting obliterated in dark clubs with strange men.

The three of us set up our area on the beach, smoothing our beach towels on the soft sand. We shared the beach with the infamous "bathing boxes"; a long row of tiny wooden sheds painted with bright colours and unique designs. Just looking at all eighty-two of them made me instantly happy. Apparently they were originally made for beachgoers to change in, and dated back to 1881. They're primarily owned by locals, and are passed down through generations; now used for storage.

Anna and I dipped into the water to cool down, and I almost forgot about my upcoming modeling endeavor. Almost.

"Would you girls be interested in getting some ice cream or frozen yogurt?" Camille asked us with a smirk forming on her face. She knew the answer before she asked it, as we agreed vehemently to the idea. We made our way to a store and joined the line-up, each purchasing our own delicious fruity flavour. As I paid for my frozen yogurt, I realized that it was the first time in a while that I'd paid for my own things. I was determined to make enough money to leave Melbourne and Camille. I felt that I'd begun overstaying my welcome, and I didn't like the way it made me feel.

Anna insisted that she come with me for safety purposes, which I accepted without protest; the truth was, I don't think I could've gone on my own. We'd done everything together up until this point, and her presence always gave me the much-needed boost of confidence to go through with our crazy ideas.

After getting off the bus, we walked around looking for the location I was given. We found ourselves entering a hotel, where we were instructed to come to a room upstairs. My mind began running wild with reasons not to go through with this photoshoot. It's just money, after all; I have a safe place to live; I don't need to travel for a year; I'm making enough money stripping; Anna isn't doing this…

I knocked on the door. A guy with brown hair and a button-down shirt answered, welcoming us in. I introduced myself and Anna, saying that she would be staying for the entirety of the shoot. After agreeing that it was fine for her to stay, he showed me to the kitchen, where he had paperwork prepared. He very briefly explained the contract, and told me where to sign. The photos would be used for his website only. Apparently they would never reveal my real name, so it would ensure the confidentiality of my identity. This was my main worry. When you strip, you're using a false identity with customers. Sure, I gave copies of my

ID to the managers of the club, but I was told they'd be destroyed after a certain length of time anyways. My true identity was a well-kept secret.

"Now, most of the girls end up coming back for a second shoot if the clients who visit our website give good feedback," the photographer told me. "Let me know if you'd be interested in that after today." It seemed a bit premature to be planning our next date, but who was I to deny the additional money when I'd reached out to him in the first place?

"Okay, sounds good," I said. I felt like a sheepish schoolgirl, uncertain of myself.

"There's makeup for you to use in the bathroom, which is just around the corner to the left," he pointed, as if I couldn't figure out which way to go. "And here's your outfit." He reached toward me, holding a one-piece black lace number. It had long sleeves and a thong bottom. I grabbed it out of his arms and disappeared from his view to collect myself in the bathroom.

I saw the makeup he'd mentioned laid out on the counter. There was an eyeshadow palette from a brand I'd never heard of. It had dark colours and the title "SMOKEYS" across the front. I attempted to darken my eyes with some of the grey colour, but the only brush available was the shit-quality plastic applicators that came with the makeup palette, which everyone knows don't work. As a result, when I changed into the lace lingerie and looked at my reflection in the mirror, I didn't really recognize myself. My nipples, while never shy, appeared to poke through the top to say hello. My face looked like a sad panda. I felt like a child who played with her mother's makeup and got caught. Fuck it, I thought, I'm already here.

We took some photos in the living room and on the bed. Then the photographer asked for me to change outfits into a teeny neon green bikini, after which we'd make our way down to the outdoor pool area. We stopped to take photos in the hallway, where I was filled with dread that a guest would come out of the elevator or their room and see this unfortunate display. I felt less sexy than I've ever felt in my life. At least when I was dancing, I could move my body to the music how I wanted. There were even moments when I felt empowered. But here, the photographer instructed me how to pose: spreading my legs wide, and removing my top to cover my breasts with my arms. I felt like an infant and a sex doll all at once; told what to do for other's gratification.

"What happened to your knees?" he inquired, noting how banged up and bruised they were.

"Oh, I'm a dancer. I recently got into it, and I do a lot of floorwork," I said, not wanting to use any terms like "exotic" or "stripper." It didn't take a genius to know what kind of dancer, though, and he was able to offer a seed of reassurance with his reply:

"Oh yeah, a few of the other girls I've worked with are dancers as well. Are you liking it?"

"For the most part, I am so far, yeah. I guess the bruises are a downside, though." I chuckled and looked down at my poor abused knees.

It wasn't until afterwards that I noticed my habit of answering men's inquiries in a way that was noncommittal and made them feel comfortable, rather than being honest. Something I'd learned to do long before stripping.

Fired

On a regular and otherwise uneventful evening, Anna had given a couple a dance in one of the side dance rooms. Apparently she let the customers feel too much of her, and the manager asked her to come downstairs to his office. He'd been watching through the security footage and saw that a hand had repeatedly gone to her groin area; as a result, she was no longer allowed to work at the club as this went against their rules. Going forward, I was working on my own, and she found another club to dance at.

Melbourne Cup

I was told that this weekend would be a busy one thanks to the world-famous Melbourne Cup. People travelled from afar to attend this event where horses raced, crowds cheered, and women wore outrageously oversized hats (so I was told). The club was preparing by asking all the dancers to work at once, and by staying open longer than usuals. My only hope was that this meant more money for me.

When Friday came around, I was at the club in time for opening, but was discouraged when I saw that there were only a few patrons in the room. I decided to take a seat near the elevator I'd just exited, refusing to exert any of my precious energy before crowds began forming.

As the evening progressed, swarms of people began filling into the small club and it was difficult to even find a seat. A young guy in his twenties came up to me, and we began chatting. I learned that his name was Chris, and he was from Western Australia. It was an annual tradition for him and his friends to make a little vacation out of the Cup. They were staying at an Airbnb nearby and were looking to have a good time. The conversation was effortless, so I ended up staying with him for the rest of the evening, drinking as we talked and laughed. I was able to go drink-for-drink with him for the most part, though I'm sure he'd had quite the head start earlier that night.

After yet another trip to the bar, we moved to sit with some of his friends. "You were sitting over there earlier," one of them said, pointing to the seat near the elevator where I'd spent the start of the evening, sitting alone and preserving energy. I nodded, as if to confirm that it had in fact been me. "You looked like a bitch," he stated crudely. I was taken aback. I'd never been told I had resting bitch face, and I certainly don't consider myself to be a bitch. "But you're not!" he decided to add, perhaps because of the look on my face.

"That's good!" I collected myself, deciding to be honest. "I don't think I'm a bitch, but I'm shy," I am shy. I left out the fact that when I'd gotten off the elevator, I had been sorely disappointed by the lack of people in the club, and had decided that rather than approach them and initiate conversation, I'd wait until it got busier and people began approaching me.

A little while later, Chris told me that he was married to a wonderful woman who he loved dearly. He also told me he fancied me and thought maybe he'd gotten married too young. Alcohol does strange things to people. As he pulled out his phone to show me a photo of his beautiful wife, a smile plastered across her face, I felt proud of his transparency and deeply saddened by his comments of possible regret. His wife was at home, he told me, trusting that he'd have a good weekend with his friends and act responsibly.

On Saturday night Chris came back and immediately asked if I wanted a drink. I welcomed the alcohol to help loosen me up for the long shift ahead, and we approached the bar.

"You're the one who tipped us so well last night!" the blonde bartender said, elated. "You're back again!" Chris smiled, and we ordered.

I felt a pang of jealousy. The bartenders were all female and done-up, looking very pretty in their black booty shorts and zip-up tops that revealed a lot of cleavage. I felt overcome with a deep-seated resentment, starting in the pit of my stomach and quickly overtaking my entire body. What the fuck, I thought. How much money did he tip them? To be fair, I'd made most of my money the night before on him, but I'd also spent hours with him, where I could have been dancing for others. I also drank a lot more than usual, which resulted in a hangover that left me exhausted and ill-prepared for the shift ahead. I felt that I'd done the hard work, entertaining and drinking with him all night, while the bartenders, who were simply overserving us beverages, reaped all the rewards.

I tried my best to repress these feelings. After all, I was overworked and probably thinking irrationally, given that I was irritated at Chris's generosity rather than grateful that he was interested in my company at all. We took a seat, and a dancer who I'd never seen before crawled off the stage to talk to Chris.

"Hey baby, like my tits?" She looked seductively at him. "Have you ever seen natural ones this big?" She took her massive breasts in her hands and bounced them up and down, as if to prove the size of them.

"Oh, yeah, they're really nice," he acknowledged, in a tone that implied he was trying to satisfy her but had no real interest.

"They're huge!" I said, because honestly, they were. They hung down low because of their sheer size and weight, and I wondered if she had back problems. If I were her, I'd certainly be looking to invest in a breast reduction at some point to reduce the stress on my spine.

Chris offered me his sweater, and like a cheesy high school girlfriend, I accepted. I zipped up his black hoodie over my bra, and I wondered in the back of my mind if this was allowed. The woman from the stage was now on the main floor because her set was done, and started pressuring Chris for a dance. He looked at me with his mouth twisted, as if he'd just eaten a lemon slice, eyes begging me for help.

"Well, I'm going to be getting a dance from Amber soon," he finally said.

"I can join Amber and we can have twice the fun!" She was really trying, I'll give her that. I didn't want her to steal money that Chris was going to give me, but I also wasn't entirely opposed to giving a dance with someone else. Plus, I'd get to feel her boobs. Chris eventually conceded, and the three of us sauntered into one of the private dance rooms. Her breasts felt very soft — clearly real.

As the end of the night neared, and people were getting more and more inebriated, Chris pulled me over to an older fellow. "This is my dad!" he sang out, overjoyed that I got to meet him. It was a moment so deeply authentic that I had to smile to myself. A family affair.

Travel

I was scrolling through Facebook — which was probably my first problem — when I came across photos of two girls I'd gone to high school with. They were in Australia too, and by the look of the albums, had already seen more of the nation in two weeks than I'd seen in my two months of being here.

"What the fuck!" I exclaimed aloud.

Anna glanced at me. "What?"

"Look at this," I turned my laptop towards her. "They're here too, and they're doing this trip along the East Coast with other people around our age."

Anna shrugged it off; she didn't seem to feel the sense of urgency that I did to explore. We'd come to Australia with the intention of traveling and meeting other adventurers like ourselves. So far, the only people we'd really met outside of Camille's house were the other dancers at the club and the people coming inside it. I was sick of it.

I understood that we'd come without much money, and that we needed to make money to do anything. It just seemed that we weren't doing anything besides working until the early morning hours (or late morning hours, depending on the day), and sleeping into the afternoon the following day. The cycle was fucking with our circadian rhythm. There's something to be said about waking up with the sun, or at least not mere hours before it sets again.

It's always sunny on social media. No one shows the truth. Everything is carefully curated to show the life that we want to present to others. Everything is always picture perfect; not a hair out of place or a blemish on the face. I'm well aware that social media isn't the real world, yet like I'm sure so many do, I still compare myself to these fake lives and unrealistic expectations.

Airbnbs

"We're going to see Curtis this weekend. He has an apartment downtown and he's letting us crash there," Anna explained to Camille one Friday.

"How do you know this Curtis, again?" she asked.

"He's a friend from university," she explained.

It wasn't entirely fabricated. Anna did have a friend named Curtis from university who was living in Melbourne. I guess the best lies often stem from a seed of truth. We just weren't intending on seeing him this weekend. We'd booked an Airbnb to stay at, so that we could work every night and rest during the day, without coming back to Camille's at ungodly hours in the morning.

A few weeks later, Melbourne threw a White Light Festival, also known as Nuit Blanche in the romantic French tongue. Anna and I actually were meeting up with Curt and some of his friends to explore, and to see some of the artistic displays of lights illuminating high-rise buildings.

As we wandered around admiring the artistic designs, we came upon an acrobatic display. The group of us watched the gymnasts leap between trapeze bars, grasping at one another. I felt completely at ease. Imagine the thrill these artists got every time they performed! The crowd cheered them on, and I felt my everyday stresses melt away.

I decided to reach out to Alex, since he'd mentioned earlier that he was going to the White Light Festival. He responded pretty quickly, saying he was hanging out at a friend's house and they'd decided not to venture into the hectic event. Fair enough, I thought.

Backpages

"I've seen you on the backpages," a tiny man told me one night at the club.

"Pardon?" I had no idea what he was talking about, and hoped desperately I'd misheard him over the loud music. I often shrugged off comments at work, dismissing the random and frequently offensive things I heard.

"I saw photos of you on the backpages for Melbourne. I never forget a pretty face," he explained. The backpages, I presumed, was where sex workers advertised their services in exchange for money. I certainly had done nothing of the sort.

I still don't know whether it was me that he saw, but in the moment, I was brought back to the photoshoot I'd done a few weeks prior, and a knot formed in the pit of my stomach. I felt queasy. It was time for another drink.

Violet

"You're from Canada, right?" the thin girl asked me. She was wearing a baggy sports t-shirt over her lingerie, sprawled out in the jacuzzi bathtub placed randomly across the hall from the changerooms.

"Yeah, I am. What about you?"

"The States," she answered plainly. "Would you do this in Canada?" she motioned with her arms a large circle around us.

"Hell no!" It was the truth; I didn't need a moment to think about it. I wouldn't be ballsy enough to do this in my own country. There was something about being on the other side of the world, knowing that a family member or friend wouldn't happen to wander in on any given evening, that made it okay. I was distanced enough physically from my old life, and it helped me distance myself emotionally, too.

She laughed and said, "Yeah, me neither!"

Turns out she went by the name Violet. She always wore a black ribbon around her neck, and black platform heels. I'd noticed her at the club before because of how she carried herself, real and raw. She had a bit of a hard edge to her, not in a tough girl, edgy way so much as a tomboy way. Seeing her lounging here in her baggy sports shirt reiterated this belief.

I only realized later that she definitely selected Violet Baudelaire from Lemony Snicket's A Series of Unfortunate Events as a character to emulate when dancing. The character in the books always wore a similar ribbon around her neck, and used it to tie her hair up when she was thinking or inventing something. Similarly to the Violet I knew, she wasn't stereotypically feminine. I read those books when I was younger and used them to escape my own life, diving into Lemony Snicket's creation. I wonder if Violet was able to do the same each night as she tied that ribbon around her neck.

We kept discussing dancing. She told me she'd been doing it for four months, and had come from Sydney.

"We're going there next week," I shared. "Any advice on finding a club?"

"Yeah, you should dance where I used to. Here, I'll give you the manager's number."

As I typed it into my phone, I realized how much I craved these connections. I'd found a friend in Louis, but I hadn't really reached out to the other dancers.

"Thanks so much! This is really helpful."

"No matter what, don't work in King's Cross," were her last words of advice. I had every intention of heeding her warning.

Health is Wealth

My diet had gotten progressively and rapidly worse. Often before going to the club, Anna and I would get sushi. I'd fill up on crab rolls or California rolls and wash it down with a bottle of Coke. The sugar gave me the energy to dance all night — combined with the abundance of drinks that clients bought for me — but eventually even that didn't seem to suffice. I saw Sophia, one of the other dancers, popping a caffeine supplement either before or during her shifts. Assuming it worked, I invested in a package for myself and began popping one before my own.

I became accustomed to working into the early (or late) hours of the morning, and then getting fast food before going to bed. One day after getting off work, I rewarded myself with a burger and fries. I unwrapped it in the underground subway station, awaiting my train. I was leaning up against the wall beside a metal handrail. As I bit into the tender meat and bun, I saw something move from the corner of my eye. Turning quickly, I was repulsed to see a rat lengthening its body out as far as it could get from its location atop the railing to get at my burger, just inches from my face. I fucking hate rodents. Rats are some of the most vile creatures on the planet. I know they're smart, and I know they can escape dangerous situations (Titanic is one of my all-time favourite movies, after all), but none of that makes them any less disgusting. My natural reaction, had I been sober and alert, would've been to throw my burger on the ground and run away. Since I was none of those things, I stuffed the remaining portions of the burger into my mouth, and took a small step back.

Shady Guys

Alex and I had become Facebook friends at some point, and I was shocked to find him tagged in photos at the White Lights Festival he'd told me he didn't attend.

"What the fuck?" I said to Anna. "Remember how Alex claimed he didn't go to the festival? Like, it's fine if you don't wanna meet up, but be honest about it."

"Ew, that's not cool."

Something didn't sit right with me. I continued flipping through his tagged photos until I saw one with a girl sitting on his lap, with a caption stating that it was her birthday celebration. At this point, I knew that he had to be in a relationship.

It's a shitty feeling when you realize you've been lied to. You feel betrayed. It's also a shitty feeling to discover that you may have accidentally hurt someone else. Alex and I had hung out a couple weeks before this and ended up hooking up. We'd made out, and I gave him a blowjob. I was confused at the time, because he came within seconds, faster than I thought was humanly possible. He'd been embarrassed, which I'd thought was cute. Turns out he was as slimy as the next guy, he'd just hidden it better.

Anna and I felt it was necessary to reach out to the girlfriend, letting her know what was up. Girl code — I would have wanted to know. I first messaged Alex, curious to see how he handled it and deciding to be honest before reaching out to the girlfriend.

Me: I was going through some photos and saw that you have a girlfriend. WTF..?

Alex: No! She's just my best friend. I don't have a girlfriend.

Me: You clearly do. I thought I'd let you know that I'm going to reach out to her because we hooked up. That's disgusting.

Alex: MISSED CALL

    MISSED CALL

    MISSED CALL

    MISSED CALL

    MISSED CALL

    MISSED CALL

Alex: PLEASE DON'T! OKAY SHE'S MY GIRLFRIEND I'M SORRY!

At this point, Anna had already typed up the message through Facebook Messenger to notify the girlfriend of Alex's behaviour. We pressed send.

She replied quickly, saying she didn't want to hear about it and letting me know she was going to block me.

I stand by my choice, because I'd always want to know the truth. They'd been together for six years. I don't know whether they broke up following his indiscretion, but I blocked him and we never spoke again.

It probably wasn't the wisest move to hang out with customers I met at work. I told myself I'd learn from this going forward.

Nudity

I firmly believe that nudity is not inherently sexual. I remember having a conversation with my housemates in university about living in a nudist colony, and the general consensus was certainly not. Only one roommate, the one who later passed away, said she'd be willing to do it to see what it was like. It would be empowering to live your life naked, where others around you are doing the same and there was nothing sexual about it. I think the rest of my friends just couldn't wrap their minds around the idea that it wasn't a sexual thing. The truth is, people who live this way aren't judging one another's bodies or checking each other out. In fact, the rest of us are the messed-up ones for making it sexual.

I recently watched a video of a professor discussing breasts. He said that most of the world thinks Westerners are gross for viewing breasts as sexual. For the majority of the world, they're simply a body part. They're necessary to feed a baby, providing important nourishment. It's only in the Western world that we've decided to make this body part a sexual thing. In truth, the only thing that is inherently sexual for humans is sexual intercourse. Everything else is constructed by humans. I think we have a tendency to forget that.

Awkward Encounters

Anna and I were still living in our Melbourne Airbnb. The guy who was renting the room to us was also living there. He didn't speak much, and mostly stayed in his own room at the other end of the apartment. Based on the photos hanging on the walls, we knew that he had a young son and a presumably-ex-wife with whom the son lived.

One morning, I finished washing off my makeup and using the bathroom after a long night of work. I was walking out of the washroom in a sleepy fog, my body feeling heavy and my eyelids already half closed, when the renter passed me to use the bathroom himself. He was up and ready for the workday, while I was clearly just going to bed.

He didn't say a word, but to this day I wonder what he thought of me.

Onward Ho!

"I'm moving to Sydney soon," I shared the news with Louis, waiting anxiously for his reply. Flo Rida's "My House" blasted in our ears — a song that will forever bring me back to this club and my early stripping days. Louis and I had grown close over the past couple of months. He visited the club regularly, but he'd never asked for a dance from me. It seemed he wasn't there for the nudity, but rather the company and good conversation.

"When?"

"Anna and I leave next week."

Yes, I broke the name rule. He already knew both mine and Anna's real names. Like I'd said before, I was a shitty stripper. I couldn't lie well, and I couldn't separate my persona of Amber very well from my own self. It didn't matter most of the time, but whenever I felt a genuine connection with someone and they asked me my real name, I told them without hesitation.

I could see the disappointment cross his face, though he tried to hide it.

"Good for you!" His words contradicted the emotion behind his eyes, but he plastered a huge smile on his face.

My last week working there was a mix of emotions. While I was extremely excited to be going to Sydney, finally exploring another city in Australia, I was sad to be leaving Louis.

On my last night, Louis said he had a gift for me.

"I'll give it to you at the end."

"Oh my god, you didn't have to get me anything!" I felt reluctant to even accept a gift from him, after all of the kindness he'd shown me and Cokes he'd bought me over the past couple months. He'd often given me some money at the end of the night just for taking my time away from other patrons, but the truth is that I always wanted to talk with him.

"Do you want a dance?" I offered.

"Oh, Cindy, are you sure? I don't want to make you uncomfortable."

I led him into the dark room, and we shared a moment of honesty, truth, and love. There are pure souls in this world, and he is one of them.

Before leaving, he handed me a small gift bag, and told me to hide it until I got to the changerooms. I did, and opened it to see a bottle of perfume by Rihanna. He knew she was one of my favourite artists. I sprayed that perfume every night before dancing for the rest of my time in Australia, and thought of Louis with a smile on my face. The job wasn't all bad.

Goodbye

We gave some nice flowers to Camille and Ken as a thank-you for everything they'd done for us. It was a small token of appreciation that felt inadequate given their generosity. I wished we could have afforded something nicer, but we'd spent a lot of the money we'd earned staying at Airbnbs in the city core when working weekends, or on food and drinks. We needed to save the rest for when we arrived in Sydney.

Werk, Werk, Werk and Twerk

We didn't waste any time, deciding to go out on our first night in Sydney.

"What should we wear?" Anna wondered aloud. "Should we be dressy in case they interview us tonight?"

We were staying in a hostel and sharing a room with six other people, but they were all out, probably exploring the city. "I guess we should be on the safe side and try to look our best," I replied.

The phone I'd used to save the number that Violet had given me had frozen and required an update. After I'd agreed to the update, it deleted all of my contacts. Just my luck. Of course, it was partially my fault for buying the cheapest phone I could find. We had to figure this out on our own.

I put on a denim skirt and a flowy top, and Anna wore shorts and a nice tank top. We threw on some cute sandals and headed out towards Violet's old club.

We paid the cover fee and went in. It couldn't have been more different from the club we'd worked at in Melbourne. There were tables everywhere, and a long stage running through the middle. The women working wore elegant dresses, no lingerie to be seen. While it was still considered a strip club, we quickly saw that this was much more of an upscale gentlemen's club than what we were used to. We asked to speak to the manager, and were told that we could interview in a couple of weeks' time.

As we left and walked down the street, I turned to Anna. "What do you think?"

"A couple of weeks is a long time to go without an income. Too long I'd say…"

"Okay, let's look up other clubs in Sydney."

We were en route to King's Cross, the very area that I'd been warned against. Google Maps revealed a handful of strip clubs within a two-street radius, and we didn't want to dismiss the possibility without giving it a fair chance. I wanted to see some of these clubs myself, and maybe hear from girls who worked there.

As we walked down the main street of King's Cross, I could sense immediately that the area itself was sleazy and gross. The air felt thick and heavy: I smelled smoke and alcohol. I saw drunks walking around, and many people who were clearly on drugs — hardened faces and tattered clothes. A neon sign welcomed everyone to see naked women. We followed it down a dark staircase. When we got to the bottom, it opened up but was still much smaller than any other club I'd been in. Everything inside was black and dark. There was a small bar to the right, and a tiny stage where a fully naked woman was doing some floor work on a white fur rug. We took a seat and watched her dance for a bit before deciding to check out the other clubs in the area.

Across the street was another club, with a red sign stating simply: Strippers. We crossed the cobblestone, ignoring a few drunk men screaming as we went. I opened the glass door to find another steep staircase. We walked down into what looked like an indoor theatre. There were rows of old-school, hard red plastic seats, all firmly cemented in place, facing the front stage. The walls were concrete and painted white. There was a girl on the massive stage doing weird stretches and aerobics, again fully naked. In the middle of the seating area was a small podium with a pole; this was the only thing leading me to believe this was even a strip club at all.

We asked the bartender, standing in front of what looked like an old concession stand in the wall, what drink options they had. It didn't look promising. He offered us a beer or mixed drink. We opted for beers, handing over the cash. "Is the manager in?" Anna questioned.

"Yeah, are you looking to work here?" was his response.

"Yes, we just got to Sydney and are looking for work at a club." Thankfully, Anna was much better in these sorts of situations than I was.

"Lemme go get him." He quickly turned and left the concession area through a back door I hadn't noticed.

Moments later another man appeared, introducing himself as Joe and offering to show us around. We followed him back up the stairs we'd originally come down, and then up another steep set of stairs going above the main level. This is interesting, I thought to myself. Upstairs, I saw what looked almost like an apartment complex. He led us into a room that had a mattress on the floor, and an open shower area.

"This here's the intercom," Joe explained. "You can call down if you need to talk to me or need help. Now, you only do what you're comfortable with."

It wasn't that Joe himself made me uncomfortable; in fact, he seemed much less creepy than Todd had in our first interview in Melbourne. It was just shocking that we had unknowingly entered what we thought was a strip club, and found ourselves in a room that was clearly intended for intercourse. I guessed this was a brothel, or at the very least, a mixture of women who danced and women who took customers up to the bedrooms.

We thanked Joe for taking the time to show us around, and we took his number when he offered it, so that we wouldn't risk being rude.

"What did you think?" Anna looked at my face to discern what I was feeling.

"Well, it was definitely different. I actually didn't mind the set-up in the basement, it felt like a movie theatre. I feel like it's nice that the seats were far away from the stage. But then when we went upstairs… Like, what the hell was that?" I trailed off.

We concluded that Strippers was maybe not the best fit for us, since we definitely didn't want to delve into the world of actually having sex for money.

We made our way down the street, and turned a sharp corner. "It looks like there's another club down here, let's take a look." Anna held her phone up to show me on the map.

The side street was far less busy. We found ourselves walking silently past houses that sat in darkness. Awkwardly placed amongst the homes was a club with a pulsing red light. The words Diamond Dolls lit up, letting us know we'd arrived. The outside of the club was covered in vines, giving life and character to an otherwise dark building. We passed through a black wrought-iron gate, grabbed our IDs from our purses, and showed them to the muscular bouncer, getting a nod to proceed.

The inside was dark, the walls covered in framed pictures and swirling gold and black designs on wallpaper. Unlike Strippers just one street over, the place exuded money and class. There was a hallway to the left and a private room to the right. We walked straight ahead and into the club. There was a long stage in the center of the room, complete with a spinning pole, seats surrounding it and benches lining the wall. The bar was straight ahead, with what appeared to be a hefty selection of alcoholic beverages. A man with swooping grey hair and a cute smile stood behind the bar, introducing himself as Noah. We asked him about employment, and he said he'd give our information to Jessica, who ran the club. I liked the sound of a female in charge, since our previous experiences had been with men. I had a good feeling about this place.

On Payment in NSW

Noah asked if we'd ever worked at a club, and we told him our story. He explained that payment at strip clubs was different in Victoria than it was in New South Wales, the state we were now in. Rather than the dancers paying immediately at the beginning of the night and pocketing all their earnings going forward, it was now all up to the bartenders. When we secured a dance with a customer, we were supposed to bring them to the bartender, who they'd pay directly. The bartender would then take a specified cut of our pay to go towards the "house," and hand us our portion at the end of the night.

The way I saw it, this system could be awesome or super shitty. On the one hand, if it was a really slow night with zero dances, I wouldn't lose money. The worst night I ever experienced was one of those quiet poker nights where I made all of $15 after a full shift. On the other hand, if I did really well, the club ends up taking a rather large chunk of change.

Noah asked us for our contact info. Since we didn't have our Australian numbers memorized, he just typed his cell number into each of our phones and called himself, explaining that he'd have our numbers in his phone and would pass them along to Jessica.

First Night at Diamond Dolls

The night after exploring the clubs in Sydney, Jessica asked Anna and me to start working on a "trial basis." She'd decide whether or not we were a good fit based on how we performed during this time. We were still staying at the hostel downtown, and got ready in our room. Sitting cross-legged atop the bunk beds we'd selected, we got out our handheld mirrors and our makeup bags. I doubt most backpackers carry around as much makeup as us, but then, I doubt they have an assortment of lingerie and stripper heels in their luggage either.

"What do you think it will be like?" Anna inquired.

"Hopefully busy enough to make some money!" I replied, shrugging my shoulders. "I guess if it doesn't work out, at least we know there are other options." The truth was, I was nervous. I don't think any situation was ever as nerve-wracking as the very first time I went on stage at a new club, with every eye watching my exposed body, waiting for me to move along to the music. Every time we changed clubs was scary, because we had to relearn what sort of clients came, what was expected of us, and who we were working with. Everything was so new.

When we first arrived, we knew to go directly to the back of the club, where we met up with the cute bartender Noah again. "Jessica will be here soon to show you around. Can I get you ladies something to drink?"

"Vodka Red Bull, please," I chimed. Not sure why I'd selected this particular drink, especially given that I was already on edge and buzzing.

Jessica was stunning. She had long black hair and tanned skin, and was incredibly fit. I would later find out that she used to dance here as well, before marrying the owner. Turns out she retired from her dancing career to be a fitness guru of sorts. She now helped manage things, working directly with the dancers. I've since heard the term "house mother"; a woman who the girls can go to with any concerns, who will help them feel safe and heard. You may be thinking Jessica was something of this sort. I guess she'd be the closest thing I ever experienced to this, but I can say with confidence that she didn't have a maternal bone in her perfectly-toned body. If Jessica was a house mother, she was a narcissistic, self-centred, and money-hungry mother who had no regard for her children's well-being and looked out only for herself.

"Come on," Jessica said. "I'll show you girls the changeroom out back." She led us to the back of the club and out a door, where we found ourselves walking on a dark cobblestone driveway. She turned left, and we were suddenly in a well-lit dressing room: mirrors on each side, chairs, and a countertop running the distance of one wall. It was smaller than the changeroom we'd had before, but had a warmer feel. There was even a clothing rack where we could hang our attire.

Jessica explained that we'd each take our turns on the stage when she called out our names. Usually this would happen a few times each night, depending on how many other girls were working on a rotation. If we were in one of the private VIP rooms, she'd skip us. I liked the idea of the VIP room, if I was ever able to actually book one of those.

"Do we have to take our tops off at the second song?" Anna asked soberly.

"No," we were shocked to hear. "You keep your outfit on when you're on stage at all times."

"What about if we get tipped up there?" Anna wanted clarification. We were both used to how things went in Melbourne, where taking off your top on stage was mandatory, and bottoms were expected if you got a hefty tip.

"Only if you get over $100 while on stage. Then you can consider it. This is an upscale venue, and we want it to look that way. If they want to see you naked, they can pay for a dance," she said without any feeling in her voice. A true businesswoman, I thought. I wasn't mad about keeping my lingerie on while on stage. It made our jobs that much easier.

Anna and I arrived a bit early to our first night of work, so there were only two other girls already there. We introduced ourselves and quickly dressed, looking forward to finishing our drinks and seeing how the night went.

Quite quickly, the club began to fill. I looked around at the rest of the dancers and was suddenly struck by the contrast to our club in Melbourne. There was hardly any diversity. In Melbourne, there were women of all shapes and sizes. Some had fake breasts, most were natural. Some had long hair, some short. Some were thin, some curvy. Here, the women were all the epitome of society's definition of "sexy"; curvy in all the right places, tanned, long hair, fake nails, perfectly plump pouts . They really did look like dolls. Each was so beautiful they could be famous for their looks alone.

Before, I'd seen customers buy dances from all the dancers. Some nights brought more success for some, but it all seemed to even out eventually. I wondered how it would go for me, surrounded by these women who fit into a much more narrow definition of beauty.

I'd just completed my first performance on stage when a man approached me.

"My friend wants a dance with you," he said. "It's his birthday, so I'm gonna buy it."

"Okay, perfect. Let's head over to the bar." I led the way.

He paid as I awkwardly waited beside him. "Where's your friend sitting?" I was eager to start dancing.

"He's near the stage, just over here." This time I followed him. He led me to where Anna was seated beside a man, talking.

"Your friend just bought you a dance! Happy birthday!" I said with a smile plastered on my face.

Anna was furious. "I was talking to him!" she screamed over the music. Birthday Boy clearly picked up on the awkwardness and sat there in silence, his mouth twisting as he fiddled his thumbs.

"His friend already paid," I explained. "Would you like to go?" I turned back to the birthday boy.

Anna was visibly upset, and repeated herself, adamant that they were busy in conversation.

There is a "stripper code," but I don't know that I was in the wrong in this case. His friend had already purchased the dance, after all. He could easily get a dance with me and resume his conversation with Anna when he got back.

Birthday Boy stood, and we went to the side hallway of dark curtained rooms. I picked one that was open and led him into it, where he sat on a black bench. The dance rooms were completely private here, which was nice.

When we finished and I came out, I looked around, but Anna was nowhere to be found. I went to the bathroom and checked my phone, where I found missed texts stating how I was a horrible friend and that I'd crossed a line. She'd left.

Jessica called Anna for her stage dance, and after no one showed, she went onto the next girl.

I took an Uber back to the hostel alone.

It's a Deal

The following morning was awkward, but I was feeling fed up with the bullshit drama that seemed to follow us like a dark cloud. I left the hostel without uttering so much as a word to Anna. I couldn't believe she'd been so selfish. When she'd asked about how much I'd made in Melbourne, she justified it by saying we both needed money to travel. When it came down to it, though, it seemed she only cared about herself.

I walked around downtown Sydney, eventually finding myself at a corner bakery that advertised coffee and espresso. I ordered myself a breakfast sandwich and an espresso, saddened when I saw how small my to-go cup was. I don't know why, because I knew it was a shot size. Last night was a disaster, I thought glumly to myself, holding my tiny espresso in my suddenly giant hand.

I came upon a park and sat down in the grass for what felt like an eternity. The words from the wise dancer in Melbourne crept into my head: "You should travel on your own... You need to do what's best for you." A part of me wanted to leave Anna. But a voice in the back of my head screamed that it would seem like I'd used her for a place to stay in Melbourne. And anyway, she was a reminder of home. I was torn, a fractured feeling that would haunt me for a while to come.

Later that day I made my way back to the hostel, where Anna was sleeping in the room. My phone rang and I answered eagerly.

"Hello? ... Yes, it's Amber... Okay... Yes, I understand... Of course... I would still like to work there."

Anna's eyes were wide as she listened attentively. Suddenly the night's events were forgotten, as she eagerly asked me what happened.

"That was Jessica," I explained. "She doesn't want you working there because you left without telling anyone. She said she can't trust you. But she offered for me to stay... and I took it."

"Oh, okay," was all she said. There was a long pause. "I'll have to look into the other places we checked out."

George

Jessica had asked me to work at Diamond Dolls five nights a week. On one of the first nights, a couple of middle aged men came in. They seemed very average and boring. A large man with a round face introduced himself to me as George. Him and his buddy went to the bar and booked a VIP room for a few hours, and he invited me to join them.

I hadn't been in the VIP room before, and was pleased to see it was pretty spacious. There were two VIP rooms in the club. This one had a door near the entrance that led up some stairs into a room that had its own little stage and pole. Running along the wall was a bench, and there were tables as well. A dancer named Harley was also invited, along with another girl named Lola. They were both tanned and attractive, but Lola was extremely curvy with breasts the size of watermelons. It was almost shocking to look at. I wondered how her back was, and if she would eventually decide to downsize the implants once she felt she'd profited enough. Her lips were so pouted that they looked like they'd hit their max on filler. Harley had a more natural look, with perfect teardrop boobs, muscular legs, and a great butt. I thought her boobs were real, as many others had stated they also did, but later found out she'd had an amazing surgeon. I got to feel them, and they even felt soft and supple like natural boobs.

Harley and Lola were joking around with the men, and the next thing I knew, one of the guys was getting a credit card out and forming lines of cocaine.

You do blow?" George asked me.

"No, I don't, but I'm not against it or anything. I just stick to alcohol!" I replied, as I chugged some more of the drink in my hand. It wasn't a lie. I drank a lot throughout my work nights. It truly helped me get by, and to deal with my anxieties and apprehensions.

"I like that," he decided, a large smile forming across his pumpkin head. "And I like you," he stated matter-of-factly.

"Thanks, I like you too," I replied, feeling accepted as a part of this odd group.

I looked over to see Lola straddling the other guy, whose name escaped me — mouths pressed together sloppily. This was definitely new.

Home Sweet Home

Since we were going to be working in King's Cross, Anna and I decided to move from our original hostel to one within that district. It made more sense; although we didn't like the area, we'd be able to walk to work instead of wasting money on Ubers every night. When we wanted to go downtown, where we felt safe and like a part of normal society, we figured that we could always venture there for day trips.

We buzzed the front desk to be let into the hostel, since the front door was locked at all times. A warm welcome to a secure neighbourhood, I thought to myself. We walked into the new hostel and found it to be quite old. It was much smaller than the one we'd been staying at before, but had a cute atrium in the center. The bathrooms were single rooms with a shower, toilet, sink and mirror. I liked those, as opposed to the stalls where it felt like your morning bowel movement was on display for all guests. There was also a communal kitchen, where all travelers could make their meals. I never did like the concept of a hostel kitchen. I'd rather have food prepared for me, even if the restaurant was unhygienic. At least that would be hidden away in the back where the food was prepared, and I could deny it to myself. In hostels, there was no denying it: the kitchens were dirty. Whenever I entered the kitchen, my nose was met with too many aromas mixed into one indiscernible, disgusting scent.

Anna and I decided to splurge on our own room, getting one bunk bed and a mini fridge. Our room was small, with a window that looked out to a narrow area between buildings. It was so cramped that I could probably reach my arm out and touch the building next to us, but the natural light and privacy was nice.

I felt like I was constantly exposed at work, so I'd begun to really crave peace, quiet, and privacy. The mini fridge quickly became stocked with drinks, as we began pre-drinking while doing our makeup before journeying two streets over to work. Anna ended up working at Strippers, and told me that some of the other dancers were quite the characters. I was happy to be working where I was.

Sister, Sister

When I began working at Diamond Dolls, I noticed that there were only a handful of us who worked throughout the quieter weekdays; most dancers came only on weekends. A massive perk of this schedule was that Jessica would order gourmet pizza for all of us to share, a thanks for our attendance in the hopefulness that patrons would choose to enter the club that night.

One of my fellow dancers was a beautiful blonde girl who went by the name Gabriella. She was from Germany and had come to travel the country as well. She'd immediately purchased her own van and travelled around with other backpackers. She told me about a group of them driving to central Australia, through the Outback, to see Uluru — Ayers Rock. They stopped and slept in their vehicles overnight, and continued on when the sun rose. It sounded spectacular.

The very first time we'd met, she passed me as I was entering the bathroom. She stopped me, face full of shock.

"I thought you were my younger sister! I was like, oh no, what is she doing here?!" she explained afterwards to Noah and me.

Her sentiment has haunted me since. I feel the same way — I wouldn't want my little sister in this lifestyle. But hearing the honesty come from her was saddening, because I realized that she probably didn't want to be here either.

Hair Tie

Harley was gorgeous, toned, and curvy, and was always so busy giving private dances that she was rarely seen on the main floor. Once, in the bathroom, I saw her tie her hair back in a high ponytail. I wondered why she did this, deciding it was probably because she was overheated. She had, after all, been in the VIP room in the back of the club all night.

It wasn't until later, when I was snorting a line of blow off a table and absentmindedly left my hair down, that I realized the real reason. My hair ran into the neat little lines, dispersing the powder all over. I felt like a moron, wasting the customer's product. I was clearly new to this.

Po Po

It was a Friday night, so the club was bumping. I was in one of the private dance rooms — which were more like cubicles, really — with the black curtain closed to give us some privacy. I was in the middle of my routine, topless, facing away from him and leaning on his lap when the whole area began to glow blue.

I'd never noticed this before, and wondered whether it meant something. I shrugged it off, since the song continued blasting and I didn't hear anyone running or screaming to frantically leave the club.

After finishing up the dance, I went back to the floor. The main room had the same blue glow. Eventually, I made my way to the bar. A customer wanted to buy me a shot, and Noah obliged, but told us that there was an undercover cop in the club. Noah had recognized him. Since Sydney had strict lockdown regulations, no one was allowed to serve hard alcohol past a certain hour. Noah informed us that he'd be handing us a regular cup with the shot in it, and instructed us each to sip it rather than shoot it, so that he wouldn't get caught.

The blue lights were to let the dancers know that there were police in the club, and to stop any illegal activity. This is like something out of a movie, I thought to myself. I wouldn't be able to make this stuff up.

You're Someone's Type

Jessica was sitting beside me, asking me how I liked the club so far. "How much did you make last night?" she asked bluntly.

"Um, like, five hundred," I replied. George had been in, which Jessica was well aware of. She knew he liked me, and his booking me in the private dance rooms was the sole reason I was doing well.

"That's amazing! Think about how much money you'll make in the long run here," she said. I was well aware of the money, although she'd happened to ask me after one of my successful nights, which were only occurring once or twice a week.

"You see," she continued, "all of the girls here are someone's type. We have the bubbly blonde," she pointed to a petite blonde dancer, "the sexy Asian," she pointed again to a gorgeous Asian girl, "and the spicy Latina," she pointed to the girl with breasts the size of balloons. I was waiting for her to continue, as I took in what she was telling me. "And," — here it comes — "the girl next door!" She pointed to me. What the fuck. Who wants to be described as the "girl next door" in a place like this? I was outraged. I smiled and said something along the lines of, "Oh, really?"

Throbbing Heart

I got into the habit of drinking Vodka Red Bulls at the club. They went down easy, and helped me stay up all night. I'd also started taking NoDoz pills, so that I wouldn't be yawning while trying to look enticing and enthralled in conversation. Eventually, I was saying yes when offered cocaine. One night I said yes to two different regulars, who weren't aware that I'd done cocaine with the other.

I got back into my hostel room that night and laid down on the bottom bunk. I felt like I was going to die. I was tossing, turning, and sweating, unable to calm down to a state where I was anywhere near sleeping. My heart was pounding so hard, it felt like it was going to come out of my chest. My blood pressure was probably dangerous, and I felt pulsing in my ear drums. I almost had a heart attack from mixing all of those stimulant substances, and if that had happened, I'd have had no one to blame but myself. By some miracle, my heart eventually calmed down, and I drifted off to sleep just as the sun began shining through our window.

*   *   *

We were in the dressing room one night when a petite dancer, who I'd determined was absolutely insane, made an announcement. "Thank god for Xanax or I'd be dead by now!" she almost screamed to everyone.

"Oh my god, I know. I need it all the time to keep doing blow," Harley agreed.

A tiny blonde dancer looked amused. "You guys are fucking crazy."

I looked on, thinking, I could have used some the other day.

Pimp

I was used to all the girls waiting at the bar at the end of the night for their payout. It was a lot different than Melbourne, where we were only aware of how well others had done on the slower nights, or when they shared numbers aloud in the changerooms. Here, we saw wads of cash handed out if we happened to be at the bar at the same time.

It did kind of feel like the bartender was my pimp, in a way, handling all of the cash for me. I also only vaguely knew how I was doing each night based on how busy I'd been, but I couldn't be sure until I was paid at the end of the evening. I didn't love this. It felt like I was being regulated by a supervisor, and as though I should be thanking him every time he paid me what I'd rightfully earned.

Ratticus

I was walking from the bottom bunk to the fridge to get myself a cold cider when I saw it. I jumped and let out a high-pitched squeal.

"What?" Anna asked, suddenly on alert.

"A rat!" I pointed out the window.

We both walked closer to the window — despite every instinct I had telling me to do otherwise — to get a better look. It wasn't moving. "Maybe he's sleeping?" Anna asked. We named him Ratticus.

We closed our window. We'd had it open for days in the hopes of getting fresh air to circulate. Boy, did that turn out well for us.

We later realized that the alleyway went to the kitchen, where this fat rat was probably feasting on all of the food it could get its grubby little claws on. I'd never been so happy to be living on an unhealthy diet of restaurant food and alcohol.

Unladylike

I was chatting with a hilarious blonde guy and slugging back beers, paid for by him, when Jessica came up to me.

"You shouldn't drink beer," she whispered. "It's unladylike." I felt the heat in my ear, and developed a sudden uneasiness at her comment, hoping she'd leave. "And don't waste your time on him," she continued, nodding in Funny Dude's direction. "He doesn't have a lot of money and won't be buying a dance, I'm sure of it."

I'm proud to say I didn't heed her advice. I was, after all, a contract worker, and if I didn't make any money from this guy, at least I'd have a good time. I figured at this point that money wasn't everything — probably a dumb mindset to have when at work where the hustle truly does correlate to how much money you make.

I cherished those beers, and my stomach was hurting from all of the laughter. And you know what? He did buy a dance after all. Fuck you very much, Jessica.

Preferences

We sat on the bench near the bar. I was on one side of this older man, and the pretty blonde German girl, Gabriella, was on the other. He'd decided to share his preferences with us, stating that he "used to love stick-thin women with large fake breasts," but that his tastes have changed, and he now prefers "regular-looking women, like you two." Exotic dancing really isn't the industry for anyone without thick skin. People think that you're giving them permission to comment on your physical appearances just because you've agreed to take your clothes off.

We nodded along, choosing to take this as a genuine compliment rather than the backhanded one it was. "If you like, I can get you a green card too," he offered. Apparently, he was a man of power and could pull this for us, if we so chose. Prior to entering this line of work, I had been extremely gullible. While I still am at heart, I have to admit that I often didn't believe a word that people spat at me when I was sitting in front of them half naked. We were both inebriated, so I shrugged it off as another hollow offer made by a random man I'd never see again.

Later that night, I left the club with one of the young bartenders, Jake, and his friends. We'd decided the party didn't need to end yet. "I saw you with Mr. Green," Jake said to me, wide-eyed.

"Uh, yeah, that old guy? Yeah, he's kind of weird." I didn't really have much to say about him. He was overall unmemorable.

"He's one of the richest men in Australia," Jake said, as though I was an idiot.

"Wait, really? He said something about getting me a green card, but

I thought it was all bullshit," I replied.

"No, he could probably pull that. Apparently his place is insane," he continued.

I was left thinking that you really can't tell when someone is telling the truth. And why hadn't he bought a dance and given me a hefty tip if his pockets were so full?

Strippers

Diamond Dolls closed earlier than Strippers, where Anna had been working. Some mornings she didn't come back to our hostel room until well after 5 a.m., when I was already fast asleep. We'd decided that I'd walk over to her work one night, and we'd head back to our place together.

I changed back into my black high-waisted leggings and teal tank top, packing my lingerie and heels in a tote bag I slung over my shoulder. I collected my earnings from Noah at the bar and emerged onto the dark sidewalk. Out of the corner of my eye, I saw a massive shadow crossing the street. It was about the size of a well-fed housecat. I'd seen this figure on other late nights, but I finally realized in disgust when I saw the long thin tail that it was actually a well-fed rat. It seemed to live on that street and, thankfully, never got in my way when I walked past in my flip flops.

I continued one street over, rounding the corner and spotting the red neon lights of Strippers. I hadn't been in since our tour where we'd seen the rooms upstairs, and I was curious to see if it was busy in the main stage area where Anna worked.

It was brighter than I remembered, not nearly as forgiving as Diamond Dolls. I took a seat, quickly noticing a middle-aged man staring at me from across the aisle. He was obviously on something, and had no shame when I met his eyes. He refused to look away. I felt far more exposed by how he was looking at me than when I was on stage in front of a crowd in lingerie.

Two young guys were sitting near me. I got up and moved beside them. I thought that maybe this would make me feel less vulnerable, giving me a false sense of safety.

The creepy man got up and made his way over to me. He mumbled something to one of the young men about moving. "Can I sit there?" was all I made out.

"Pardon me?" The young guy was confused.

"Can I sit there?" he repeated, now pointing at the seat, in case there was any confusion.

"No, you cannot. I'm sitting here," the young Aussie continued, glancing at my frightened face. "I'm sitting here with my girlfriend. Please leave."

They say heroes come in all shapes and sizes, and I was grateful for mine that night. The old man didn't want to leave, and swayed about for what felt like an eternity. He finally returned to his old spot.

"Oh my god, thanks so much," I said sincerely. "That was terrifying."

"What the hell are you doing in a place like this?" I explained that my friend worked there, and I'd just gotten off work myself a street over. Now that I looked at him, I could tell that he, too, was on drugs.

The announcer's voice rose over the crowd. "Mickey, everyone! The beautiful Mickey!" Anna took the stage, and I turned to the guys, letting them know that she was the friend I'd mentioned. They cheered for her so loudly! I was still shaken but managed to find their enthusiasm endearing.

After Anna's stage performance, she came out to the main area and we left. I never stepped foot in that place again.

Peter Pan's Travel Adventures

Anna and I were walking down the main drag of King's Cross when two young blonde women in jean shorts stopped us. "Hey, are you girls travellers?" they inquired.

We told them that we were from Canada, and had been in Sydney for a few weeks. They invited us to a party at a place called Peter Pan's Travel Adventures, where they said they worked. It was just down the street; we were to show up later that night. Apparently they hosted a weekly party night to get backpackers together, and would be providing the ever-evasive goon beverage we'd heard about, but never had the pleasure of tasting.

"Okay, we'll see you there!" Anna said, accepting a pamphlet from them.

We continued walking. I was ecstatic at the idea of meeting other young people like us. I still felt like we hadn't gotten to experience the true backpacking lifestyle, and wanted nothing more than to meet others and have some lighthearted fun.

Piercing

Later that day, we walked closer to downtown Sydney. "I think I want to get my septum pierced," I voiced aloud.

"Wow, really?" Anna looked at my face, assessing whether or not I could pull it off. "That would be cool," she determined.

"Really? You think it would look okay on me? I feel like I need change."

"Yeah, let's do it today!"

So we did. I'd already had many piercings in my life. I liked the impermanence of them, that you could remove them at any moment. Not like a tattoo, something I don't think I'd ever be able to commit to.

We were both off that night, but rather than have a quiet night for once, we pre-drank in anticipation of meeting other backpackers. Sitting in our hostel room without a time limit, doing our makeup seemed fun instead of arduous. We weren't getting dolled up to go to a club and put all of our energy into a facade. Amber and Mickey could rest; we were going to be ourselves tonight.

I followed Anna into the travel agency, which was decorated primarily with yellow — such a happy colour. We made our way in and found it was absolutely packed with young people like ourselves. I felt like I was getting a breath of fresh air after being held underwater for far too long.

We approached a table where there were huge bowls filled with some sort of punch. "Goon, my ladies?" a cute guy asked. He was tall and slender with auburn hair and scruff on his face.

"Thanks!" I held out a red Solo cup for him to fill. He handed us a piece of paper. "C,an you both write down your names and phone numbers?" he asked, pointing to the pens on the table. "Every week we do a draw for a prize, sponsored by Peter Pan's Travel."

We both nodded, taking the paper and quickly jotting down our information as instructed.

"Rad piercing," he added, pointing to my nose.

"Thanks, I actually just got it today," I blushed.

"No worries, it looks great on you."

Another guy, quite a bit shorter than the first, walked over and introduced himself as Chad. "You girls have never been here before, eh?"

Anna and I both shook our heads. He had a mischievous twinkle in his blue eyes, making me wonder what he was up to. We found a place to sit, and one of the blonde girls who'd invited us began yelling out to the crowd.

"Now for the main event!" she screamed. "The winners of the trip across Australia!" This news was followed by cheers and applause from the crowd, obviously more familiar with what was going on than we were.

They called my name. I stood up in shock. Wait, what? I thought. Had I won?

"Are you here?" the girl shouted.

"Yeah," I said in a normal volume, and walked over to her.

When she recognized me, her face lit up. "Oh, you came! I'm so happy! And you won, — that's awesome. You'll have to come back in someday to arrange the trip."

I was elated to have won something! Although I had no idea what the trip entailed, it was exciting to think that money might not be an obstacle to me seeing more of this massive country. Between the goon and the prize, I was riding a high that night amongst my fellow backpackers.

Sadly, my regular, George, had a different opinion regarding my new look. "You don't look like yourself. You're changing; I don't like it," he stated bluntly, staring straight into my eyes in the dimly lit room. Interesting that he should think I care.

"I just wanted a change!" I said, pretending to be much more chipper than I was feeling. "I can always take it out, anyways. It isn't permanent." I hoped this would suffice, and that he wouldn't hate it so much that he'd stop requesting my company in the private dance room. He was my main source of income, after all. Without him, my time spent at Diamond Dolls wouldn't be worthwhile.

Excluded

Some nights at Diamond Dolls, important customers came in. By important, I mean well-off, and by well-off, I mean known by the dancers for being generous with their tips. We were all sitting around on a quiet night when a large man walked through the doors. All my coworkers swooned. "He's here!" they all cheered, unable to contain their excitement, and beelined for him the second he tried to sit down.

Seeing as the club was nearly empty, I followed them and found myself sitting on the outside of the circle. The girls seated directly beside him were stroking his arm, speaking in cooing high voices. This disturbed me, since I knew this wasn't how they naturally spoke.

He told us all to choose a drink, and Noah served them to us on a tray. Just then, I was called to the stage. I could tell that they were engrossed in conversation, with no eyes on me. When I was done, I went to sit off to the side with a couple of younger guys, and the petite blonde girl was called to the stage. While I was seated across the club from Mr. Money Bags, and the blonde girl was dancing, I watched in silence as the entire group stood up and walked out. They stopped at the bar first for more drinks, and then made their way to a VIP dance room. The blonde girl didn't hide her alarm. Her mouth dropped open as she realized that the seat she'd previously been in with the group would be empty when her set was done. I felt bad for her - it truly was just shitty timing.

I felt bad for myself, too, because I'd made the choice to sit elsewhere. I hadn't continued to ogle Mr. Money Bags as if he was the hottest thing since sliced bread, which he certainly was not. All I know is that all those other girls did very well that night, and I left without much money to show for it.

Straws are for Sucking

"Could we get a straw, mate?" One of the regular customers, Brad, yells over to Noah, who passes him a black plastic straw from behind the bar. I'd explained to Brad that my nose was still tender. We made our way to the woman's bathroom and entered a stall together. He lined up the coke on the reflective toilet paper dispenser and took a snort. Sniffing, he handed me the straw. "Here, give it a go." Genius, I thought, and followed his lead.

Appearances are Everything

I've always felt that whatever you're praised for the most throughout your life becomes your primary identity. Students who perform well in academia are often rewarded and called "smart"; this often becomes a self-fulfilling prophecy as they internalize this identity and strive to succeed. People who are deemed "athletic" strive to uphold this name for themselves. Those who are called "beautiful" focus on their outward appearances. This isn't true for everyone, of course, but usually the pattern holds.

As a result, I've found that the most naturally "beautiful" people — based, of course, on society's standards of the word — are often the ones who do the most extra work to look good. How ironic. I wonder if the women who spend their lives stripping feel that looks are all they have to offer. I imagine the longer you stay in it, the more challenging it could be to separate yourself from this identity. I wasn't in it long enough to find out.

When I was young, Disney movies showed me gorgeous and elegant princesses who were kind to others, and ugly and evil villains who fought them. In Snow White and the Seven Dwarfs, the Evil Queen gazes at her reflection in the mirror and asks, "Who is the fairest one of all?" When the mirror replies that Snow White is the fairest, the Queen orders her killed out of jealousy. It's heartbreaking to think that the entertainment so many of us watched as little girls portrayed a message where women were competing againstone another out of vanity and envy. Why is it that the Beast in Beauty and the Beast was forced to live in the body of a monster that we consider "ugly," but is transformed into a handsome man at the end? What message does this give children about our outward appearances? I hope that movies and books going forward reject these ideas. How messed up is it that we're telling impressionable children that looking a certain way is directly correlated to one's character?

Are you Brazilian?

There was a power couple in the house one night. Again, everyone else seemed to know who they were, except me. She was a sexy young Asian woman and he was a very mediocre middle-aged white man. She came up to me at one point, and we began chatting.

"Where are you from?" she asked, genuinely curious. "Are you Brazilian?"

"I'm Canadian! But originally a mixture of things, like Irish and Ukrainian," I explained, realizing I was oddly flattered by her guess. Some of the women who I worked with were Brazilian, also on Working Holiday Visas, and one thing they all had in common was that they were stunning.

"Oh! I wasn't sure with your dark hair and curves. You're beautiful," she continued. When a man tells you you're beautiful, you accept the compliment, but take it very much with a grain of salt. That's even more intensified in a strip club because most of the men have beer goggles on and are paying for women to get naked, therefore seeing all the dancers in a sexual manner the moment that they enter the club. When a woman tells you you're beautiful, especially this woman who stood before me, glowing and badass with tattoos and winged liner, you graciously accept the compliment. I beamed, feeling truly beautiful inside and out.

She asked me to follow her to the VIP dance room, and I began walking behind her to the space I typically only ever entered with George and his friends. When we got to the door, her husband said loudly, "I've already got someone." I saw a short brunette wearing white beside him, ready to enter the room. Husband and wife began whispering to one another. Eventually the three of them left me standing there awkwardly, wondering what was going on.

Later that night, I heard the other dancers in the dressing room talking about how the brunette had gone home with the couple and how big of a deal it was. Apparently, once you're "in," you have the potential for major earnings, the watermelon-breasted girl announced. She seemed jealous. Or perhaps she knew all this because she had experience, I surmised. I couldn't be sure.

At the end of the night one of the young bartenders named Nick invited me to join him and his friends, including Brad, to an afterparty of sorts. I accepted willingly, wanting to make friends who were my own age and not paying me for their company. They offered me some blow, which I also accepted, although it stung a bit when I snorted it. I'd been told that it was hard to smuggle drugs into the country, and as a result, a lot of them were laced with cheap filler. I thought back to that when I snorted my second and third lines, trying to ignore the stinging that reminded me of snorting milk out of my nose as a child.

"So what happened with that couple tonight, eh?" Nick asked me, digging for gossip.

I told him what had happened, and finished by shrugging my shoulders. I tried to play it off like it didn't bother me, but anytime you knew you were close to making a hefty sum and it slipped through your fingers, you couldn't help but get a bit annoyed. Excluded again, I thought to myself. Although the reality was I don't think I would have gone home with them anyways, it would have been nice to have the option.

Stereotypes

"You aren't like the other girls here. You're different." If I got a dollar for every time I heard this phrase, I'd be rich. I'd usually inquire as to why the speaker thought this, and the answer would be something like, "You're just not the typical girl who gets into stripping," or, "You're smart and educated," or something else along those lines.

What is the stereotypical girl who gets into stripping, anyway? A broken, uneducated, drug-addicted woman just looking for her next hit? I'm sure some strippers are like that, but the women I met were all different. Some were students, paying their way through university by taking off their clothes. There were mothers who worked a regular, "vanilla" Monday-to-Friday office job and wanted to supplement their income. There were those of us travelling who found freedom in this unique lifestyle, making money as we went. Everyone had a different story, and I always found it interesting to hear the strange preconceptions that patrons had about who would be entertaining them that evening.

When we believe what others tell us about ourselves, we risk losing our own identity. My biggest fear is forming a concrete opinion of who I am, unable to transform as I experience different things in this vast and expansive world.

Boobs Pre-Boob Job

"Can you ask one of the guys back there if they'd be interested in having me dance for 'em?" the tiny blonde dancer with round breast implants asked me, wide-eyed. "Not your guy! But I was talking to the other one earlier," she explained, reassuring me that she wasn't breaking stripper code. She'd stopped me on my way between the bathroom and the VIP room to ask. I was in there as usual with George and a couple of his friends.

"Yeah, sure, I'll ask him," I nodded my head. I'd barely spoken to this girl before, and didn't feel particularly obligated to follow through. She was in the main dance room when I returned. I sat beside her to catch my breath. As we were drinking, she pointed to my natural, unexceptional breasts and said aloud to no one in particular, "Your boobs are exactly like mine were before I got my boob job! Exactly!" I chuckled because I didn't know what else to do, and she continued. "Pre-boob job twins!"

This girl really was tiny: she couldn't have weighed more than ninety pounds soaking wet. Although I'm typically content with my body, her comment rubbed me the wrong way. I don't know if she had any ill intent, but I suddenly felt a bit sheepish about my lack of excess breast tissue.

Keep 'Em As Is

There were men who told me directly that I should never get fake boobs. They enjoyed a natural bosom, and didn't want me to feel pressured to change myself to fit a stereotype of what is considered beautiful. While I appreciated the sentiment and ego boost, these were the same men that paid me for my company whilst I was naked. Their heartfelt compliments didn't count for much.

Coke, "Not the Drink"

A week or so after I got the new piercing, George invited me into the VIP room with a larger entourage than normal. I was informed that they all knew one another because their children were in preschool together. I couldn't help but wonder what their situations were at home and if their wives knew where they were. We all went into the back room, and it immediately got wilder than a regular night. The men asked to do lines of coke off our bodies, flashing the cash they promised if we obliged. I ended up doing a line off one of the girls, and for the price of $100 also let someone snort a line off me.

Noah came back to ask for a drink order, and paused for a moment to look at me with concern. "Like what ya see?" George slurred. "She's beautiful, take it in," he continued unnecessarily.

"Yes, she is," Noah replied, then brushed off the comment and addressed everyone, "Would anyone like a drink? Orders!" Everyone ordered, and he vanished as quickly as he'd come. The three other girls were taking turns on stage to entertain the customers, but since I had no ability on the pole I sat with them and continued drinking and chatting.

"What's your price?" one of George's friends asked me.

"Pardon?" I was confused. Hadn't he just handed me $100 to do a line of blow? I guess that's my price, I thought to myself.

"To come home with me. What's your price?"

Oh… "I don't have one, sorry. I don't do that," I replied, turning down the request gently to minimize the risk of offending his ego and being kicked out of the VIP room.

"Ah, you're killin' me. I like you even more now!" he chuckled.

Interesting.

I realized I had to pee, so although the last thing I wanted was to get up and attempt to walk in that state, I was forced to try my best.

"Are you okay?" one of the bouncers asked me with a concerned look on his face. I had just stumbled out of one of the private dance rooms in the club. I nodded my head signifying that I was fine, although the honest answer would have been far more complicated than that. I made my way down the stairs and through the dark hallway that followed, arriving in the bathroom. I looked in the reflection and barely recognized myself in my coked-out haze.

When I made my way back to the VIP room, I decided to clamber on the small stage, since it now sat empty. I got up there and started some floor work, the guy who asked me my price staring intently. As I took off my white lace underwear, I saw that something white was stuck inside the folds of my vagina. I glanced down and noticed a clump of toilet paper that I'd carried with me from the bathroom. In a movement that I hoped looked graceful, I quickly stroked my leg towards the toilet paper, grabbing it and tossing it on the ground. The man was still watching. Fuck.

I got tired of the stage and made my way back to the bench where the guys sat. George had stepped out to take a phone call, so I began dancing on the lap of my latest suitor. I threw my head down, wanting to look sexy. I smashed my face in the process; apparently there was a table in the area that I hadn't been aware of. "Oh my god, are you okay?" the man asked, mouth agape.

"Oh, yeah," I grinned. If I hadn't been high, I'd have been embarrassed. But given the circumstances, I just reached for my face to see if there was any blood. None to be found. It continued to sting for a while, but I continued to party, which worked as a band-aid for a while. I had a black eye for a few days. It paired nicely with the nose ring to make me look kind of badass, a word no one had ever used to describe me in my entire existence.

High School Acquaintance

Over the months I'd worked at Diamond Dolls, I'd spent a lot of time with George. He came in at least once a week, asking for a private dance every time without fail. I began relying on this money, since the reality was my earnings fluctuated greatly. Some nights I left with $60 in my pocket, but when George came, I often left at least a few hundred dollars richer.

One night as we were talking, he shared the reason that he'd initially been drawn to me: I reminded him of someone. "You bring me back to a different time," he said sincerely. "A long time ago there was someone really special to me in Greece." I could see in his glassy eyes that these memories danced like ghosts. He'd really loved this woman.

It felt like we shared a moment. I was well aware that he was paying for my time, and readers might think it odd that I felt a pang of sympathy and compassion. The best way to describe our relationship was that it felt like we were high school friends. You know the ones that you're only friends with because of the circumstances, and the moment that you're handed your diploma, your relationship ceases to exist? It was like that. He was one of the only people that I spent time with on a consistent basis, so I felt some sort of connection to him, however circumstantial it may have been.

Bartender

Noah was another constant presence, working the bar every night. There were a couple other younger bartenders who helped out, but Noah clearly ran the show. When Jessica wasn't there, he was in charge. He was kind, and always treated the dancers with respect. I'd seen George offer him cocaine before, but he always turned it down, explaining that he had a "bad heart." I'd grown to respect this man and was curious about his story.

I eventually found out he'd been a full-time teacher at a private school, moonlighting at the club for extra cash. He'd recently left the teaching profession altogether, turning to the club for full-time employment.

One evening, a short redhead who often came into the club and was friends with another bartender, was having a drink with me. Brad was chill, joking around with the girls regularly. He came a couple nights a week, enjoying the atmosphere and presumably the views, but chose to spend his money on drinks rather than lap dances. We sat in the corner of the club near the bar. He joked about his meaty pecs, which were looking larger than my boobs that evening. I was wearing the black bra and underwear that I'd purchased in Melbourne with the light pink embroidery along the edges. In my defense, it had very little padding and didn't give me any lift. The truth is that my breasts were far from huge. I laughed along, joking that he had a handful, and we went on to grab one another's chests to compare.

I caught Noah glancing over from the bar, trying to hide a questioning look on his face. After Brad left, Noah came over to me. "What was the boob grabbing all about?" he asked.

"Oh, we were just trying to measure who's were bigger," I explained, as if that made the scenario any less strange.

"Well, if you ever need help with that after hours, I'm always available," he said with a cheeky expression on his face.

I made my way through the darkness back to my hostel room, unable to shake Noah's comment from my mind. I was interested in him. I wanted to get to know him beyond the interactions we had at the club.

I recalled the very first night Anna and I had wandered in, how he'd called his own cell from my phone. I opened my cheap piece-of-shit cell and went through the history, finding an outgoing number I didn't have saved in my contacts. Now or never, I thought. I typed in, "Does the offer still stand to measure my boobs?"

I waited nervously for a reply, realizing that he might flirt with all the girls. Maybe this was his way of trying to create a working relationship. If he didn't respond, I'd have to show up at the club again and endure the awkwardness that I'd created, knowing I'd been rejected.

My phone went off. When I finally brought myself to look at it, I saw his response: "I'm almost finished up here. Want to come to my place?" My whole body exhaled in relief as I realized the interest was mutual after all.

I got out of the Uber and walked in the darkness to the address Noah had texted me. When I got to the entrance, he came to the door to greet me, leading the way to his apartment. It was an old brick building with a homey interior. When Noah opened the door to his apartment, I saw a rather small bachelor pad. There was a little kitchenette directly ahead of the door and a living room area on the left, which was furnished with a couch and a glass table. To the right was a bed that pulled down from the wall. Further to the right was a door that I presumed led to the bathroom.

I barely had time to take it all in. The door closed behind me and Noah leaned in for a kiss, grabbing me by the waist. There was a lot of passion behind that kiss, and I felt myself melting into it as we made our way to the bed. He undressed me and we made love on the bed, discovering one another's bodies and sharing ourselves entirely.

Afterwards, when we'd moved to the couch and began talking about our lives, he confided that he'd been engaged in the past.

"What happened?" I inquired, curious about his history.

"It was just kind of a realization I had. I was going away with a buddy on a vacation and just realized…" he trailed off. I waited patiently, thinking to myself that this was probably a painful memory for him. I couldn't imagine being close to marrying anybody; wanting to spend the rest of my life with one person was a foreign concept to me.

Noah continued. "I realized I didn't want her to come with us. I just wanted to go with my friend. But I knew that I probably should have wanted her to be there." He looked into my eyes earnestly.

"That's fair. So then what happened? You called it off?" I wanted to hear more details, more about him and his life before I'd met him.

"Yeah, I came back from my trip and called it all off. It was hard, ya know, but I think it was the right call in the end."

I glanced away, nodding in agreement. My eyes fell to the glass table, and I noted the pill bottles with prescription labels adhered to the sides. I guess he'd been honest when he told George he had a heart problem.

Noah

Another evening, I spent the night at Noah's place. As we sat together on the couch, I told him about my sisters, one older and one younger.

"Thank God for middle children!" he exclaimed — which in hindsight really pissed me off, because he implied that I was playing into the "rebel" middle child stereotype. I despise the notion that I'm predictable.

We began talking about the club, and I asked him if people went beyond dancing there. "I know people make out, but does more happen?"

"Well, I've found used condoms in the private rooms a few times," he explained. I wasn't shocked, after all the things I'd witnessed.

"At least they're being safe and using protection!" was all I could think of to say. "What about you?" I wondered.

"What about me?" Noah didn't know exactly what I was getting at, so I clarified. "Have you been with any of the dancers before me?"

"Ah, well, yes. I have."

"Many?" I was curious, but also felt suddenly self-conscious. I didn't know if his prior relations meant more, and maybe diminished what we shared.

"Two," he said. "The first one was tough. I really liked her. We began seeing each other, and I was falling in love with her." I tried my best to listen without allowing my own feelings to overtake me. Rationally, I knew that our relationship was our own and not to be compared to others. In the moment, though, my feelings were a bit hurt thinking that he'd been with other dancers before me.

"I eventually found out she was working at a rub-and-tug," he said sadly, his voice lowering. "Would you do that? Do you feel like it's different from stripping?"

"I wouldn't do it. Not because there's anything wrong with it, but to me it feels much more intimate. Dancing is already hard enough for me, honestly," I responded.

"She said that it wasn't any different than taking her clothes off for money. It was just an act for her, using her hands." He seemed to drift away.

"I don't think it's fair to keep that from someone you're seeing." I felt protective of him. I could see that this woman had betrayed him by keeping this secret from him. She had been the first person he was vulnerable with since his fiancé, and she'd cut him deeply.

"That's how I felt. But when I told her that I was upset, she got defensive and said I was being ridiculous," Noah continued. "The relationship disintegrated quickly after that."

I realized that for some, sex work is work. There isn't a line that can be drawn in the sand from what they deem intimate and what's just good business. Noah explained that this dancer felt dances were even more intimate at times than hand jobs, and although I've never worked at a brothel of any sort, I can see her point. It depends on your perspective, I suppose. While most people would say that stroking someone's genitals is quite personal, talking with customers about yourself and your life over the course of several drunken hours is an act of baring your soul.

Into the Rabbit Hole

Not all exotic dancers were like that, though. Some were able to come into the club presenting an illusion, keeping conversation with patrons minimal. One of the most successful dancers at Diamond Dolls did just that. Valentina often showed up after hitting the gym, with her sweaty hair back in a ponytail or bun. She'd change from sweatpants into her red lingerie, throw on some mascara and scarlet lipstick to match, and hit the club floor. She never spoke to customers for long, and was frequently found giving lap dances.

To this day, I'm in awe of Valentina. She barely drank — something that was incomprehensible to me — and seemed to reveal nothing about herself or her life outside of the club. I admired her greatly. She certainly did well financially, and was much healthier than myself. I imagine this is the only way that a dancer could work long-term without compromising their health too much. Unlike Val, I was completely myself. I wished I could put on a sexy persona, but it felt unnatural and unattainable to me. I wonder if some people are just better at compartmentalizing their lives: fitting certain topics into boxes and leaving them at the door when stepping into their other roles.

Bondi Beach Day

I was getting irritated again at the lack of sightseeing that Anna and I had been doing. Sydney was a gorgeous city, with a tropical feel and waterfront that transported me immediately into a blissful state, but we still hadn't been to Bondi. "We should go to Bondi Beach," I said to Anna one day. "Some of the girls at Diamond Dolls were talking about how they do this trail walk from Bondi to Coogee Beach. Apparently it's along the ocean and just stunning," I offered.

"Okay, let's take the whole day tomorrow and do it. We can get up earlier than normal to explore the area, too," Anna agreed.

So it was settled. We'd finally get to see the infamous Bondi Beach! I was elated.

The next morning, we packed a bag with towels, bikinis, and sunscreen. It took us over an hour and a half to get to Bondi, since we had to take multiple subways and then transfer to a bus to reach the destination.

The journey was well worth it. As soon as we got off the overcrowded bus, we found ourselves moving within a large swarm of people, walking in unison from the bus stop towards the beach. The street was bustling. Some people came and went from the shops that lined it, and others ran across the street carrying surfboards. There were houses all along the cliffs that bordered the ocean, with what one could presume were unparalleled views. I could smell the saltwater and feel the carefree joy. This is what Australia was supposed to be.

"Wanna change into our bathing suits and lay in the sun for a bit?" Anna asked.

I was all in. The turquoise water seemed to me far superior to the dark lakes I was accustomed to in Ontario. We found a store with a bathroom we could use (a surprisingly difficult feat in Australia) and changed into our bikinis, ready to hit the beach. We walked over and paused to admire some rad graffiti artwork. Facing the water, I noticed that there was also a swimming pool located to the right of the beach area. I was confused as to why anyone would use the pool when they could swim in the ocean instead, but to each their own, I figured.

"Here's a spot!" We laid down, relaxed into our towels, and scanned our surroundings. "I wanna take my top off so I don't get tan lines," Anna declared.

"I mean, I'm all for it if no one's around or we're at a nude beach," I paused to look around. "But there are kids here."

She undid her top while lying on her stomach, but had the courtesy of covering her nipples while laying on her back, so as not to upset any families. I wondered whether she'd always been this way, so completely unashamed, or if the industry had altered her perspectives on nudity. I never asked, and I never found out.

When the heat became unbearable, we realized we needed to cool down before starting our walk. "Want to go for a dip?" I suggested, shielding my eyes with my hand as I scanned the horizon. I saw dozens of people surfing, but no one was swimming close to the shore. Odd, I thought.

"Definitely!" We left our things on our towels and walked towards the water, passing other avid tanners as we went. I felt pale in comparison to most of the people we passed; my pasty Irish ancestry skin can only get so dark. We both waded eagerly into the water, immediately feeling refreshed. Within seconds we'd made it far enough to immerse our entire bodies.

The waves were intense, crashing into the sand — and into us — with a ferocity I hadn't noticed from the shore. I started kicking my legs and swimming towards the sand, and realized in horror that I wasn't moving. If anything, I was getting pulled further away.

"Why can't we get back to shore?" I yelled to Anna.

"Oh my god, I noticed the same thing!" she screamed back.

We both swam hard, eventually finding an angle that brought us back to the comfort of the sandy beach. As soon as it was shallow enough, I rose to my feet and ran out of the water.

"Fuck, that was terrifying," I gasped.

Anna agreed. We walked back to our towels. I felt a bizarre mixture of embarrassment at my reckless behaviour and my underestimation of nature's strength, and gratitude for escaping before things got worse. I was hit with the realization that the pool was beside the beach for good reason.

When I told my mother that we'd gone to Bondi Beach, strategically sheltering her from our struggle for our lives, she messaged me jokingly asking if Hugh Jackman had saved me from the water, as it had recently been in the news that he'd had to save someone else at this very location. Little did she know how very close to reality that was.

On Accents

The strangest thing happened as I travelled the country. The more people I had the pleasure of meeting, the less I could distinguish between their different accents. Before leaving Canada, I could hear someone speak and, at the very least, know if they were Australian, British, or Irish. As I went on my merry way around Australia, they all melded into one. It was as if I could only differentiate between Canadian/American and "elsewhere." It was the very opposite of what I thought would happen, and to this day I struggle to tell what accent someone has.

Paranoid (by Ty Dolla $ign)

When we'd gone to Bondi, I'd noticed that there were outdoor gyms placed along the walkway area. They basically included an assortment of metal bars, both vertical and horizontal, where the "outdoorsy" gym-goer could work out while also getting their vitamin D.

One night I was getting ready for work in the changerooms at Diamond Dolls when I overheard this scenario:

Pretty brunette # 1: "He's so hot. We're going on our first date tomorrow. I'm so excited!"

Pretty brunette # 2: "That's awesome! Where are you going?"

Pretty brunette # 1: "I'm not sure — he's picking the place."

Pretty brunette # 2: "Well, don't sleep with him on the first date! Make him work for it. Where'd you meet?"

Pretty brunette # 1: "We met here at the club. He asked for my number one night. He's always down by Bondi, working out…"

Pretty brunette # 2: [pause] "Wait, what's his name again?"

Pretty brunette # 1: "Dylan… Why?"

Pretty brunette # 2: "Is this him?" [shows a photo on her phone]

Pretty brunette # 1: "Yeah, that's him… Wait, what? You know him?"

Pretty brunette # 2: "We're seeing each other, that piece of shit… Girl! Don't trust him… Oh my god, I can't believe it."

Girl who had no place interrupting the conversation: "Oh my god! I got two bad bitches in the club, and I know they know about each otherrrrr…"

Yes, she really started singing "Paranoid" by Ty Dolla $ign. I made my way out of the dressing room, feeling like nothing could shock me anymore.

Australia Backpackers Facebook Friends

Anna and I had joined the Facebook group for Australia Backpackers, where others who were travelling abroad posted things like jobs, ride shares, and places to see. We tried to peruse the webpage frequently enough to feel like we were truly a part of this group, despite the irrefutable reality that we were not.

I thought it would be a really cool experience to pick fruit at a farm. Backpackers often worked for a few months, befriending their comrades, and were provided room and board in exchange for their labour. I envisioned myself sitting around at the end of a hard day's work with my feet resting on a chair, caked in dirt and my own dried sweat, sipping on a cold beer with my fellow workers. We'd discuss our old lives, the reasons why we found ourselves here, and our dreams for the future.

The stories I read on the Facebook page, however, warned about employers taking advantage of travelers, withholding proper compensation, and, in many cases, getting away with it because there were too many legal hoops for backpackers to jump through in order to fight it. Other posts consisted of gruesome images of swollen hands, with captions stating that a spider with a name out of a Marvel movie bit them while picking fruit.

It was on a day when Anna and I each had some time to scroll through this page, trying to avoid the stories of fruit pickers being hospitalized and the stresses of manual labour going virtually unpaid, that we came across an advertisement for a day trip to the Blue Mountains, located about an hour's drive from Sydney. The ad said that the company, calling themselves the "Travel Trio," consisted of three young guys who were native to Australia, but had spent the past few years travelling around the world. Upon returning home, they figured they didn't want to stop meeting like-minded young people, sharing new experiences, and seeing new places. They started their own company, where they could continue to meet people with these same aspirations and show them the sights that their local region offered, all while making money and living the dream where work felt like fun.

We were sold. I privately messaged the guy who had posted the ad, stating that my friend Anna and I were interested in going on their next day trip to the Blue Mountains, and asking how we were to pay. Within a couple of hours the whole thing was set, and we were ready to meet other backpackers for a fun adventure.

The day finally came, and Anna said she was feeling too sick to join. We had both lost the fight against a brutal cold and were still a bit stuffy, but I was too excited about the trip to opt out. I decided I'd take some Paracetamol and be fine to partake in the day's adventures alone. I got ready and hopped onto a bus to the address I was provided, which was downtown at a different hostel.

When I got there I saw immediately that the central location was bustling. The hostel itself was buzzing with backpackers and excitement; this was the kind of feeling I wished we had at our hostel.

"You here for the Travel Trio Blue Mountain trip?" a thin girl with short hair asked me. I nodded, suddenly unsure if I was outgoing enough to do this on my own.

At that moment, an Australian with short golden hair announced to us all that his name was Blake, and that he was one of the tour guides. "My mate will be bringing the bus 'round for us all to hop on. I'm just gonna call out names first to see who's here!" It seemed almost everyone was accounted for, besides Anna. As promised, a big white bus lurched to a stop in front of us. There were stickers plastered on the sides, and as we boarded I saw that the personalized decorations didn't stop there. There were knick-knacks hanging from the rear-view mirror, and Blake tossed around some wigs and sailor hats for willing backpackers. He himself wore one of the sailor hats. As we pulled out of the city, they had the music blasting, and everyone was keen to share stories and get to know one another.

When I saw the view, I knew I'd made the right choice in coming. The Blue Mountains were breathtaking. A wide expanse of trees stood before me on rolling hills as far as I could see. There was a blue haze hanging above the trees: Blake and the driver, Seth, explained that it came as a result of eucalyptus plants emitting an oil that, when mixed with dust and water vapour, looks blue to us.

"Eh, you guys wanna head down there?" Seth pointed to a trailhead, already populated with hikers coming and going. "It takes ya to the Three Sisters," he continued. We all nodded eagerly, wanting to see as much as possible.

We walked along the stone path and down many metal stairs until we came to a rock formation consisting of three large stones above us. Everyone began taking photos. The plaques explained that the rocks were made of sandstone, and had been created by erosion 200 million years ago. The names of the three rocks, the sisters, were Meehni, Wimlah, and Gunnedoo. The plaques went on to explain the Aboriginal legend about the three sisters of the Katoomba tribe in the Jamison Valley. A tale of love that could never be: the three sisters fell in love with men from a neighbouring Nepean tribe, but due to tribal laws, were forbidden from being together. The men captured the three sisters, which began a battle between the two tribes. An elder from the Katoomba tribe turned the three sisters into stone to protect them but died in battle, unable to turn them back.

I thought of my sisters back home. I thought of the experiences that shaped us and of the women that we had become. Both of my sisters have always been gorgeous, both inside and out. My older sister is tall, blonde, and blue-eyed, with skin that tanned easily. She'd been told her entire life that she should model or become a volleyball player. Much like me, she loathed the notion of being told what to do, so she travelled and worked abroad in over sixty countries, and then went back to university to become a lawyer. She loved shocking people.

My younger sister — who looked like she came out of an old Hollywood film, with large waves in her chestnut hair and a rounded, youthful face — was more sensitive. She wasn't sure what she wanted to do career-wise, but was studying the sciences, which she found fascinating. She liked meeting new people and said she'd figure it out as she went.

Growing up, we'd moved around and changed schools a few times. While this was incredibly difficult, especially throughout puberty and high school years, I think it brought the three of us closer together. We knew that no matter who we met at school, we'd come home and have each other.

We stopped at a bottle shop to purchase some adult beverages, since we were going to a park for a BBQ lunch.

"Have you ever tried kangaroo?" Seth asked from the large grill, positioned permanently under a roof area for all-weather meal preparation. To my surprise, a few people said they had tried it, but opinions on how it tasted ranged greatly. This made me all the more eager to have some.

"Eh, it's all about how it's been prepared, though," Seth explained, looking at his kangaroo dish — presumably prepared in the proper fashion. We sat around on the grass, talking about what hostels we were each staying at and how long we'd been in Australia. I had mounting feelings of shame over the fact I'd been there for months at this point, far longer than some of the others, with very little adventure to show for it. I felt again that the life I'd been leading was not what I'd come to this country to do, and by working five nights a week, I didn't leave myself the time or energy to do what I wanted during the day.

Seth doled out portions to those of us who wanted to try the kangaroo dish. Although the meat itself was dark and a bit tough, he'd cut it up into bite size pieces and barbecued it in a sauce that almost made you believe it was moist. There was a mix of veggies tossed in with the meat, which also seemed to take away some of the gameyness of it. I finished my plate and washed it down with the ciders I'd bought earlier. I quite enjoyed it, though I certainly had no intention of replacing chicken, which I ate frequently, with kangaroo dishes in my diet.

Blake and Seth instructed us all to pack up and board the bus again for our final stop — a waterfall that they promised was a hidden gem. "I don't have a bottle opener, does anyone have one?" one of the girls a few seats up from me called out.

"Ask one of the Germans, they can open bottles with anything! I'm always impressed," Blake replied. Sure enough, one of the German backpackers accepted the challenge, taking the bottle from the first girl's hands and tilting her plastic water bottle upside down. She lined up the caps, and with the flick of her wrist, the top popped off. Simple as that. I was impressed, too.

It was weird descending the bus stairs on a back road, but Seth said he'd drive around and find a place to park it while we began the trek. Blake led us through a forest and down a slope. After what was probably only fifteen minutes, but felt much longer with our anticipation, the trees cleared to reveal a large waterfall that cascaded into a pool of water. Seth took his tank top off and jumped in, whooping as he went.

On the ride back, the music blasted, and my head began to thump along to the beat. I could feel the ciders and the Paracetomol wearing off. The tour guides told us that they'd only been doing day trips so far, but they were really excited to be planning their first ever longer trip up the East Coast. They'd be taking a group with them and driving from Sydney up to Cairns over the course of about a month. They'd camp along the way and stay in hostels. I want in, I thought to myself.

You Can't Afford Her

I'd been in a private dance room with a drunk middle-aged man for a few dances, and our time had come to an end. I guess it was a slow night, because as it ended, Noah showed up asking if he wanted to purchase more dances with me.

"If I wasn't working, I'd love to be in your spot," Noah said to the man, trying to convince him for my sake. "She's beautiful."

"Eh, she is," the man slurred, "but you couldn't afford her."

Oh, the irony. I thought to myself. He's getting all of me in exchange for his company.

Slow Nights

It was a slow night, midweek, the type of night where Jessica occasionally bought us pizza as a treat. The girls and I were all standing around by the bar, sipping on free drinks generously offered by Noah. I imagined he felt bad that we were working and no customers had walked through the doors since we'd opened. I stood beside Gabriella, the pretty German backpacker with golden ringlets. We were all lined up, leaning against a chrome bar that was attached to the benches in front of us.

Finally, a small group of guys sauntered into the club, taking a seat near the stage. All of the other dancers immediately beelined towards the men, eager for the opportunity to make money. I took another long sip of my drink, sighed, turned to Gabriella, who was the only other one remaining, and said, "Ugh, I guess I should go over there." I sounded extremely depressed, not unlike Eeyore in Winnie the Pooh. She burst out laughing, and we made our way over to them together.

That's the moment I realized I was over this line of work — and the moment I realized that the best thing to come out of it were the relationships I'd formed and the memories we shared, however fleeting they may have been.

Needles

It was a busy evening when I saw a flash of something that scared me. I was almost unsure, and questioned whether my eyes were deceiving me.

I was speaking to a group of young men who'd come in, evidently in the middle of some pretty intense partying. They were sweating and talking loudly, which I didn't think much of because it was crowded and the music was blasting through the speakers, creating a vibration I could feel in my chest. I myself often found I was perspiring in the club, having to wipe sweat off my brow.

"Eh, I might get a dance with this one here," the dude I'd been talking with said to his mates.

I was ready to secure the dance, trying to lead him to the bar where Noah was waiting to take his payment. It was like controlling a kindergartener whose attention wandered as soon as you had it. He was standing back with his friends, so I followed. I saw a guy hand him a needle, which he quickly hid.

Oh. I know I've spoken about cocaine and a lot of drinking that I'd participated in — even overindulged in — but needles like that one have always made me nervous. There is just something so much more intense, so much more malicious, about injecting substances directly into your veins.

Many of my friends have a fear of needles, regardless of their intended use. I don't share that view, since I've embraced piercings, deliberately paying people to poke holes in my body like I'm a piece of Swiss cheese. No, for me needles are all about tricking your mind and body. The effect is supposed to flood your body with a warmth I've heard described as an immediate whole-body hug, an embrace that comforts you when no one else can. I think I would love it. And that's what scares me the most.

Shopping Spree

In order to balance out our wild nights, Anna and I often walked around the city, browsing storefronts and eating at patios during the days. We made a concerted effort to get up before noon — a difficult feat for anyone whose schedule allows them to get to bed no earlier than 5 a.m. — and forced ourselves to get outside, enjoying the sunshine. As someone who's suffered pretty severely from Seasonal Affective Disorder, I think these days were one of the only reasons I was doing remotely alright at this point in time.

We decided to escape King's Cross by walking downtown, which always breathed new life into me. I felt cleansed when I got to escape that ratty place. There was something deeply disturbing about being there in the daytime. It was as if the darkness of night cloaked the filth, and when the sun shone, it revealed the foulness. In the daylight I was no longer able to refute it.

I was on the hunt for a lipliner, and had heard great things about the longevity and colour range of MAC's liners. "Hey, Anna, can we head to MAC?" I voiced my thoughts aloud.

"Yeah, for sure. I always like to browse," she agreed.

We found ourselves in a large department store with a variety of makeup counters. I'm not the biggest fan of these counters, since the individuals working them are constantly pushing products down my throat and patronizing me as if I'm a child playing with her mother's makeup for the first time. Since I already had a good idea of what I wanted, I made a hurried decision of a shade that might suit my dark hair and slight tan. The lady stood on the other side of the glass counter. She was quite a bit older than me, her makeup making her resemble a porcelain doll. "Is that all? Can I suggest a lipstick to pair?" She opened her palm and moved it gently towards the lipstick display.

"No, thanks, that's all," I said awkwardly, unprepared to spend more than the $30 I was already forking out on an unnecessary product. She rang the purchase through and handed me a small black bag with my new pencil in the shade Whirl. I hoped it would look good on me, and would earn me money.

I found Anna browsing the lingerie section. "I'm going to try these on," she said, holding up a number of items draped over her arms. While I awaited her emergence from the changerooms, I began to peruse myself. For every item I inspected, my mind immediately inquired as to how easily I could remove it, whether it would look sexy coming off, and how easily I could get it back on. I recognized that this was not how I'd used to think about lingerie. It was always something to make me feel good about myself, and maybe something to provoke someone else to take it off me before getting intimate. These qualities no longer mattered; it was simply a costume.

We wandered into a number of other stores, and I found myself carrying more and more bags. I bought an assortment of tops, and a pair of black platform sandals that I didn't need.

After spending insane amounts of money, I felt my stomach gnawing at itself. "Let's get something to eat soon, I'm starving," I suggested.

"Me too, oh my god. All this shopping has given me an appetite," Anna agreed.

We soon found ourselves at the gorgeous harbourfront. The aquamarine water calmed me down immediately, and I slowed down my pace as I held onto that fleeting feeling. "Oh, look, there are some restaurants along here," Anna pointed ahead. I'd been in such a daze, transfixed by the water that I'd neglected to look for places to eat.

"Perfect! I love that there's seating in front of the harbour. Let's see if we can get in." We walked directly to the hostess at the entrance. Decked out in a black outfit and sleek hairdo, she inquired about our reservations.

"We don't have anything booked. Do you have any openings?" Anna asked.

"For just the two?" We nodded our heads in unison, crossing our fingers. The smells wafted into my nostrils and I just about melted. This is fine dining for sure, I determined.

"I actually have one table for two, a late cancellation," she offered with a smile on her face.

"Oh my god, that's perfect!" We were thrilled. Two seats just for us — it was meant to be.

We followed her to the table, taking a seat outside on the cobblestone patio covered by a rooftop in case the now sunny sky suddenly turned rainy. I examined the menu and decided on a cocktail and a pasta with oysters. After placing my order, I went to the bathroom, where I decided to take a roll of toilet paper. Our hostel bathroom frequently ran out of thin, scratchy, tissue paper–like rolls. I don't know what possessed me to do this; I'd just gone shopping, spending hundreds of dollars on clothes and makeup.

"I took a roll of toilet paper to hold us over a bit longer before we buy some," I explained to Anna when I sat down.

"Wait, you..." She burst out laughing. "We went on a shopping spree today, and we're sitting at a gorgeous high-end restaurant, and you decide to take... toilet paper?!" she couldn't contain herself. She was right that it hadn't made any sense at all. If I could afford to lead a luxurious lifestyle, I could certainly afford my own toilet paper (double-ply at that!). I joined in laughing.

"Hey, if I'm spending this much on dinner, I think I've more than paid for the toilet paper, too!"

The thing about having an inconsistent income, making so much money some days and hardly anything on others, is that my state of mind was just as inconsistent. I fluctuated between living like I was on my last dollar and like I was wealthy, rarely finding balance in the middle.

The Proposition

We were in the back VIP dance room when I explained to George that I still had debt from school. This wasn't intended to be a great revelation, rather an honest admission that might explain why I was where I was. "How much do you owe in student loans?" he asked, his eyes boring into mine in the dim lighting.

"Um, like twelve grand–ish," I replied.

He was quiet for a moment, stroking his stubbly chin while pondering my predicament.

"Well, I can get rid of that for you if you want to hang out sometime."

I desperately wanted to do that. I wished with every fibre of my being that I could take him up on his offer. I knew what he was insinuating, but the rational part of me thought, One time to erase all my student debt wouldn't be so bad, would it? I found a way to reply without giving a definite answer, hoping to keep the option open in case I got the nerve to take him up on the offer.

I thought back to the conversation I'd had with Noah about his ex. I felt like there was a line for me, and accepting the proposition would be crossing it.

Disillusioned

As the nights progressed, I became more aware of all of the negatives of this job. The aspects that once seemed glamorous were now largely overshadowed with the grimey and demeaning realities. The darkness crept into my being. I was like an alcohol-consuming vampire, tired and out-of-place in the daytime and resentful at night. It had gotten to the point where Anna and I felt it was necessary to drink before setting foot in our respective workplaces. We simply didn't want to be there.

One night I found myself beside one of the other dancers who also happened to be from Canada. "Whereabouts in Canada are you from?" I inquired, hoping to stretch out my conversation with her rather than put on an exhausting facade with a patron.

"A town in Quebec, just across from Ottawa," she replied with ease.

"Oh, my older sister lived in Ottawa for a while." I was excited to have even the slightest connection with a stranger while on the other side of the world. "How long have you danced?"

"For like a year at this point," she replied. "My Working Holiday Visa is coming to an end soon."

"I don't know how everyone does it," I said, suddenly sobering up. I paused. "I feel like everyone else is fine working here, but I'm just so exhausted. I don't know how long I'll last to be honest."

She looked at me with her bright blue eyes. "I need to take a holiday like every couple of months."

"Really?!" I was shocked. I'd never heard anyone admit to feeling the same way as me. It seemed like all the other dancers thrived in this environment, whereas I was slowly deteriorating into a shadow of my former self.

"Yeah," she continued. "I have a vacation booked in two weeks, and I'll need to start organizing my next one as soon as I'm back just to get through." I realized that I wasn't alone in feeling the way I felt.

I wondered if I appeared to be having a good time to everyone else. I wondered how deceiving our outward appearances could be to how we were actually feeling inside.

Name Your Price

"Everyone has a price!" said a guy in his twenties. He was giving off extreme douchebag vibes only enhanced by his white t-shirt and the chain strung around his neck. I sat wordlessly on one side of him, with the feisty dancer on the other.

"No, I don't think so! I get paid to dance," she rebutted, hopeful she could change his mind. I could already see that it was a lost cause.

"Oh, everyone says that until they get offered a high enough number. I bet everyone in here would sleep with someone if the price was right." He was cynical, thinking that money was the driving force of everything. I'm not sure why I didn't just get up and walk away. There weren't many people in the club; it was a slow night. I guess I was curious where this was going. I was certainly disgusted by this man and his conversation, but a part of me wanted to hear his thoughts. They were clearly so vastly different from my own, and isn't that how we develop empathy — by listening to one another? Or so I'm told.

Strong

While onstage, I relied on my thick thighs and large derriere to get attention. I'd developed a routine of sorts, where I'd eventually take to the floor and do some provocative movements, and occasionally the splits — something I certainly shouldn't have been doing since injuring my knee, but while intoxicated was proud I could do. By no means was I talented on the pole, so I avoided it for the most part.

One of the girls at Diamond Dolls, petite with dyed black hair, was incredible on the pole. When she went on stage I was always in awe as she climbed up and twirled down, moving at dangerous speeds. She was always dripping with sweat by the time she got off stage.

"I'm self-taught!" she declared one night in the dressing room. "I just started foolin' around and tried different things on stage. I learned all my moves that way," she continued to tell the other dancers. I was impressed.

One night in the VIP room, Harley told me she could teach me some simple maneuvers. I wanted to learn. I felt that I should at least know a few tricks for the stage, since I could only do the bare minimum on the pole after months of stripping. "You can definitely do this," she stated matter-of-factly.

She held onto the pole and began walking, lifting herself while twirling around gracefully, moving her legs in a slow, controlled manner through the air. When I took to the pole to try it, with only Harley, George, and his friends as witnesses, I failed miserably.

"Hoist yourself with your arms," Harley instructed, as if saying it could magically give me the upper body strength needed to perform the trick. I attempted it again and struggled to get the air needed to really spin around the pole. She tried giving me instructions a couple more times, but I gave up before I lost all dignity.

Cruisin'

"We should go on a cruise!" Anna declared one day while we were at the hostel, lying around with our computers.

"I'm listening," I said, awaiting the whole plan. Anna was the planner of the two of us, while I was game for most things.

"Okay, so there's this island called New Caledonia. It's a French island, I believe, but it's near Australia and a popular tourist destination, I guess. I was looking into it, and we can get deals for, like, $700 a week.

If you think about it, that's accommodation and food for 7 days at $100 a day, which is definitely less than we're spending now for everything."

She knew perfectly well I'd be down. I was getting so burnt out from work, and a getaway of any sort seemed like a dream. "Here's one for $730 each," she continued, pointing to a deal online. "It isn't the best cruise line, I don't think," she hesitated. "I don't know… I was just thinking outside the box, ya know?"

"No, I love that idea! Anything to get away. And being on a cruise ship enjoying the sunshine and relaxing — that seems like just the thing," I agreed. "We can look into different deals and plan for it in a few weeks or something, to give us something to look forward to. And then hopefully we get to do that East Coast trip that the Travel Trio were talking about." It almost felt like a lie to classify us as backpackers, but I so desperately wanted to be one.

We found a cruise that was neither luxury nor "cheap." We'd get a room on the interior, assuring ourselves that we'd be spending our time on the deck anyways. The pricing was double if you wanted a drink pass, which provided you with bottomless drinks for the duration of the trip; Anna and I agreed that our livers could use a weeklong vacation, and that we could purchase the odd beverage if we wanted for the usual additional fee. We both knew that if we'd paid the extra $700, we'd feel obligated to get our money's worth, which would lead to bad choices and overindulgence.

We bought the tickets and were set to go cruisin'!

Shrek

I am not a tiny girl, but I am not a curvy girl, either. I am somewhere in between.

I was having a drink with a group of young guys one night, and chatting with the one closest to me. We got along well. If I'd been out for a night on the town and started talking with him organically, I would have continued the conversation, which was a rare thing to find at my workplace.

"Your hands are so big!" He pointed to them, as if I didn't know where they were despite having had them attached to my body for twenty-three years.

"They're like Shrek hands!" He laughed a little too hard at himself. I chuckled along because I was taken aback and didn't know what else to do, and because I'd enjoyed his company up until he made this comment.

"They're not tiny, I guess," I agreed, though I also thought the comparison to the green swamp character may have been a bit uncalled for.

He got up to join his friends, who'd gone to the bar to get refills. When they came back, they each asked a girl for a private dance.

"Want to dance for me?" I was shocked because of his Shrek comment, and the fact that I thought we'd been teasing each other in a sibling kind of way.

I led him to a private room, taking his hand in mine.

I Quit

"I'm going to be leaving in a couple weeks," I told Jessica, knowing full-well that she wouldn't be pleased to hear the news. She knew I was a backpacker, and was stripping to earn money for my travels, but I hadn't yet worked two months at Diamond Dolls. Besides, she'd had me working five nights a week because I was a newcomer to the club, and needed to put in my time on the slow weeknights. She'd now have one less dancer sitting around for potential customers.

She stared back at me, processing the information. "If I'd known you'd be here for such a short period of time, I would have let your friend stay."

I don't know if she thought that comment would anger me, but I was happy that Anna hadn't been allowed to work with me. The distance was needed: it eliminated a lot of the drama between us. I shrugged and walked away.

No Exit

One evening, I decided to take a quick break from the hectic atmosphere in the club. I made my way to the dancers' dressing room out back. I'd been talking with a couple of young guys who were probably doing more than drinking, based on their functions. As I passed Noah, I noticed that the men were following me. I quickened my pace outside, walking as quickly as I could over the uneven ground in my seven-inch heels. I hoped that maybe they'd turn around when I entered the dressing room. Maybe they were confused and in search of a restroom, I thought to myself, trying my best to ignore their footsteps behind me. They followed me into the bright dressing room, through the only door. I suddenly realized I was trapped. Now the two of them stood there, a muscular barrier between me and the door, my only exit.

Within moments, I heard a man's voice: "Hey, you're not allowed in there." It was Noah. He repeated himself and one of the guys quickly apologized. They turned to leave, and I stood there in shock.

"You okay?" He examined my face earnestly.

"Yeah, thank you." I was so relieved. I don't know what the men were planning on doing, but whatever it was, I wouldn't have had the physical strength to stop it.

I recognize that I was extremely fortunate to stay safe throughout this time. I never had anyone follow me while I walked through the pitch black streets back to my hostel, or threaten me in any serious way. I'm beyond grateful for this, and would be the first to admit that I wasn't necessarily taking the precautions I should have to keep myself safe. I was naive, but lucky, too.

Hair Down Under

Most of the women I worked with chose to remove their body hair entirely, leaving their vaginas naked and smooth. They either waxed, lasered or shaved the hair away — whatever was their preferred method of removal. I myself shaved, simply because it was the most cost effective and convenient way at the time. I was unable to commit to regular appointments and didn't want to spend much money on my appearances, something that proved to be rather challenging while I was in this line of work.

Some women opted for cute landing strips, neatly trimmed and maintained. There was one dancer, though, who left her bush alone, free and untamed. She got just as many dances as the rest of us. I wish I'd gotten to know her. She seemed like the kind of woman who refused to abide by society's unspoken expectations, living her life being unapologetically herself. I'm still working on that.

Capital Bound

We'd boarded the train in a station that reminded me of Platform 9 ¾ in Harry Potter, with brick walls and large clocks. The train we now sat on was much more modern than the Hogwarts Express, and moving along at a decent speed. We were headed to Canberra, the capital of Australia. As we veered out of the city into the countryside, I wondered what the capital would be like.

Anna and I had planned to stay at a hostel, but sadly were still unable to fully fund these adventures, so it wasn't going to be all fun. We'd looked into it and found a couple of options for work, none of which were that close to our hostel.

From a tourist's perspective, after visiting Melbourne and Sydney — both of which boast oceanside beaches and city living — the appeal of inland Canberra was pretty much nonexistent. We were going mainly to say we'd seen it.

When we got there, the first thing I noticed was the more rural feel. We hopped in an Uber and directed the driver to the hostel. We drove alongside a river with a lot of greenery, which reminded me of home.

We arrived at our hostel, checked in, and found our way to our room, unloading our things and each taking our bunks. I didn't want to think about work, since Anna and I had decided to take the first night off and get some sleep.

The next morning we rose a bit after the sun, and decided to walk around the area. It felt good to explore as a true backpacker rather than as a stripper — at least, until we started dancing again in Canberra. We found a grocery store and purchased a few supplies, passing a nail salon as we perused.

"Anna, how would you feel about getting a manicure or pedicure? I would love to treat myself to a pedicure, and God knows my feet could use the love. Plus, then they'd look good for our cruise!"

"I'd be down to get one," she agreed. We asked the women if they had any time for a walk-in and found that they did, to our delight. I opted for a coral colour, which I felt gave the illusion that my skin was more tanned than it really was. It was a happy colour, carefree and cheerful: two things I'd been feeling very little of those days.

After our morning adventures, we found ourselves back at the hostel in the common area. "What do you recommend for us to do in the short visit while we're here?" Anna was asking the other travellers.

"You have to climb the mountain!" an elderly man said excitedly. "The best time to do that is either at dusk or dawn, because that's when the kangaroos are on the move."

Thank God for connections — I'm ashamed to say I didn't know anything about this mountain or the kangaroos. We thanked him and decided to make the journey later that day. Early mornings didn't really align with our schedules, after all.

Kangaroos

"Ready?" Anna asked. I nodded, agreeing that we should get going before we missed the sunset altogether. We bought a bus pass and used Google Maps to hop off at what we thought was the correct spot, near

Mount Ainslie. Turns out we'd gotten off far too early, and were lost in a random neighbourhood. We wandered the streets for a while, nervous we were taking too long. You can't fight nature, I thought.

"Okay, there it is!" I pointed to a sign that informed us we were on the right route.

"Perfect!" Anna replied.

We marched through the bush with all the confidence we could muster, until we eventually got to a path that was cleared. Walkers and joggers began passing us, filling us with relief that we were finally where we were supposed to be.

We'd been walking for a bit when out of nowhere, we heard a whoosh and saw a brown blob whiz rapidly past us. "What was that?" we said, looking at each other for answers. It happened a few more times before we realized that the blobs were kangaroos making their way down the mountain. The more kangaroos hurtled past us at lightning speed, the more our anxieties started creeping in. At one point, a rather large kangaroo stopped on the path and stared us down.

"Um, what are we supposed to do?" I averted my eyes, unsure if we were supposed to treat them the same as a bear. Up until this point, I'd always compared kangaroos to deer; docile and doe-eyed, gingerly eating grass in the fields. Now that this massive animal stood in front of me, I saw that it was nothing less than a beast. Its muscles rippled through its skin, and I wondered whether they were known for being aggressive towards humans. We were actually both so concerned that we took the time to research on our phones, finding to our dismay that they could kick us into oblivion.

"Okay, let's just pick up the pace and keep our eyes down so we don't threaten them," I determined as we moved up the mountain. "What if they don't see us? They're just popping out of the trees so fast they might accidentally knock into us," I worried.

"There are still tons of other people walking and jogging without any worries. I'm sure we'll be fine," Anna tried to appease me.

We were so distraught with the kangaroos that we somehow found ourselves lost. We weren't sure what direction to head in next and were trying to decide when we saw a red truck coming down the road.

"You girls lost?" A man poked his head out of the truck, slowing to a stop.

"Uh, yeah, we aren't sure where we're going," Anna said, abashed at our carelessness.

"Well, where do ya need help gettin' back to, Los Angeles?" He burst out laughing at himself. Anna and I looked at one another, then down at ourselves, realizing we probably looked ridiculous in our jean shorts and tank tops, with our large sunglasses to top off our outfits.

"We're actually from Canada," I explained, now sitting in the truck behind him. He'd generously offered to take us into town, where he'd said he was headed anyways.

"Canada!" he exclaimed. "I'm a firefighter. I was there a couple years ago to help out with the wildfires you guys were having in the Western part of the country," he offered.

True to his word, he brought us into town. We thanked him for the drive, and for helping our country with the forest fires. We decided we'd earned ourselves a nice dinner to calm our nerves, and I'd decided that kangaroos weren't so cute after all.

"This place looks nice, wanna check it out?" I wondered aloud, pointing to a restaurant that gave off a lovely ambience. It was on a corner, and had windows all around the outside. I could see wooden floors, wooden walls, and people seated at tables, deep in discussion. Outside, string lights hung above a patio. The temperature was dropping rapidly now that it was getting dark. I shivered as I realized how grateful I was that the firefighter had found us on the mountain when he did.

Anna agreed that the restaurant looked inviting, and we found ourselves seated eating pizza in no time.

Lustful

We'd found a club in Canberra with good reviews and had decided to check it out that evening. Anna and I had a few ciders in our hostel room before venturing out, taking an Uber to the seemingly random location. We drove out of the city center and into an industrial area, full of large boxy buildings that resembled factories.

"Here ya are," the Uber driver stated. Stepping out of the car, we found ourselves at one of these large boxy buildings. I never would have guessed it was a strip club if it weren't for the pink neon sign declaring the contents to be Lustful. We thanked him and made our way up to the building. I felt uneasy at the location. The clubs I'd worked at in Melbourne and Sydney were downtown, with shops and people bustling around them at all times. This club was far removed from the city. It was the sort of place where someone could disappear without a trace.

I relaxed when we stepped inside. It had the typical strip club vibe: dark, of course, with stages, seating areas, and a well-lit bar. This venue was much larger than any of the other clubs I'd seen.

Anna and I walked to the bar and bought a drink, telling the bartender that we were here to inquire about work. He said the manager would be out shortly, that she was just in the back getting some things together. Another female in charge, I noted.

We wandered over to sit by some dancers. The women had weird animal face masks on; apparently it was a themed night.

"We're looking to dance here," Anna explained. "Is it a good place to work?"

"Yeah, it's great," said one lion-dancer.

"I like it too. I've been here for a while now," a zebra-dancer added.

A forty-something-year-old woman appeared and introduced herself as Audrey, the manager, shaking our hands. She told us the basics. We'd have to go on the main stage throughout the night: the large circular stage placed disjointedly off-center in the room. There would always be an employee at the entrance to the private dance room to take funds from the customers. We'd then be paid out at the end of the night. It was a no-touching club — that was new. It all sounded good, though, and we agreed to start the following night.

Low

Since we were planning to take an Uber home, Anna and I decided to take public transportation to work on our first night to save some money. We gave ourselves adequate time to prepare, which entailed pre-drinking and doing a full face of makeup. We sat in our hostel room sipping on some drinks and making up our faces, hoping that Lustful would make us fistfuls of cash.

"I'm gonna mix a drink to take for the road," Anna said, pointing to an empty juice she'd had earlier that day.

"Great idea." I immediately decided to do the same.

As we sat on the bus bench waiting for our ride, I felt my apprehension and nerves begin to calm. I sipped my drink. Minutes later, we boarded the bus and were on our way to our new place of work.

Anna and I made our way to the back dressing room, where I applied my red lipstick. I usually went for a more nude colour, but occasionally spiced it up with a bright red, which I felt looked good with my dark hair. I never had the courage to wear a red lip in my everyday life, so I liked to take the opportunity at work. I looked at my winged liner and red lips in the mirror, and decided that it would do. Alcohol combined with makeup and lingerie always gave me a false sense of bravado. I put my heels on, turned to Anna, and asked if she was good to go out.

"Yeah! Let's go straight to the bar and see if we can convince the bartender to give us a free shift drink," she said.

"Sure, why not?" I agreed, though I was already feeling the effects of my numerous pre-drinks and the roadie I'd had on the bus.

"We don't normally do that," the bartender said somberly to Anna. She managed to coax him into it, saying that we were nervous for our first night. He made us each a drink and we left him alone, taking a seat at a bench on the floor.

After a while, we started drinking with some customers, conversing about Canberra and our visit so far. They were young, and the discussion flowed easily.

"Can you come back to my office to chat?" Audrey asked Anna and I a little bit later. We looked at one another with blank expressions. I had no idea what she wanted to talk about. She led us into a back room.

"You were letting the clients touch you," she stated bluntly. It was not a question. I was confused, because we hadn't even had private dances yet.

"Pardon?" I felt a knot form in my stomach, unsure of what was happening.

"The men you were sitting with had their hands on your legs. The other girls told me," she clarified, as if that explained everything.

Anna and I were both lost. All I wanted was to go back out onto the dance floor and leave this awkward encounter. The manager standing in front of me had seemed like any other business owner the night before, but had transformed into a very intimidating woman, making me feel like a schoolgirl getting scolded for something I didn't remember doing.

"Oh, okay. I didn't even notice," I muttered. It was true that we'd come from Sydney, where touching was the norm. Of course, no one was supposed to touch your genitals, but I'd witnessed even that on numerous occasions. And the managers always turned a blind eye when money was being made.

Anna and I agreed to be more cautious going forward.

"And you," she continued, pointing to Anna, "I'm cutting you off. You've had enough to drink." Sure, we were both intoxicated, but that was the nature of the job. I wasn't used to feeling controlled or patronized by management. We left the room shocked.

The night progressed, and I began noticing the other dancers giving us dirty looks. When I took my turn on stage, I got tips like I'd never seen before. In my experience, the stage was where you'd try to gain attention in order to get private dances later on in the evening, but it appeared that here in Canberra you could actually make a decent amount of money up there. I was pleased at that.

I got a few private dances, and I admit that I became very drunk as patrons bought me drinks. At one point during a lapdance, the guy started feeling me up. Two girls in the dance room yelled at me, so I moved to the floor to dance safely in front of him. As I eventually moved back onto his lap, however, his hands again went up my leg towards my vagina. I guess I didn't stop it soon enough, because the next thing I knew I was being hauled back into Audrey's office.

"Pack up your shit and go!" she spat at me. "You're done!"

I was really fucked up, so all I could think to do was laugh. I went to the dressing room, got all my things together, found Anna, and told her I was kicked out. I got my cash and left the club. I took a cab back to the hostel and stumbled my way into the shared kitchen. The drinks had caught up with me. Since I'd always had drinks before work at Diamond Dolls, I figured my alcohol tolerance had become superhuman. This night proved otherwise. I scoured the fridge and found someone's leftover pasta, devouring it as though it would erase my shame, as if it would sober me up.

The next morning I threw up pasta with whole chunks of mushroom, confirming that I barely chewed a bite.

Local Guide

Despite the fact I only worked part of the night, I still made hundreds of dollars. I was jealous that Anna had stayed and made about twice as much as me, but I recognized that I'd fucked up by allowing touching when there were strict policies in place.

I'd given my number to one of the guys who'd come into the club the night before. Alessandro was a bit older, somewhere in his thirties, and lived in Canberra. From what I recalled — which admittedly wasn't much — he seemed like a nice guy. I remembered him offering to show me around the city. Sure enough, he messaged me asking what I was doing that night, and I explained that Anna would be returning to the club but I wouldn't be. He said he'd love to take me out and show me around, if I was interested. Fuck it, I thought, I'd might as well be having fun if I'm not making money. And so I agreed.

Anna had just left for the club when I walked out of the hostel. "Wanna see Canberra lit up at night?" Alessandro asked me as I climbed into his truck.

"Yeah, that sounds nice," I nodded, excited to be on my own adventures that didn't involve working.

We drove to the Mount Ainslie lookout, the same place where I'd experienced the terrifying kangaroo incident. I told him the story and he laughed, but he agreed that kangaroos are not as cute as people imagine. When we got to the top he offered me a beer, which I declined due to the hangover from hell that I'd been nursing all day. He sipped one as we looked out over Canberra. It was gorgeous lit up at night. I was glad I'd accepted his invitation, and was surprised at the level of comfort I felt with him. Usually when I was with a man in a first date type situation, I wanted nothing more than to escape, but with Alessandro I was just immediately at ease. We talked about the city and my travels, and I learned that his family was originally from Spain. He was tall and confident, without being cocky.

He drove me around the city and took me out for tacos at a place downtown. Then he asked if I wanted to go back to his place. I surrendered to my curiosity; the night had already gone so well, and I wanted to see what would unfold.

Alessandro's place was a clean bachelor pad. We took a seat on the couch in the living room and he put on a show that neither of us were into. When he leaned in to kiss me, it felt like we'd done it before. It was comfortable, like wrapping yourself in a favourite blanket or wearing an old cozy sweater. It heated up quickly and he carried me to his bed, where he undressed me and kissed down my body. The heat from his mouth made its way down as he pleasured me with a ferocity of someone who genuinely cares about his lover's joy. We made love like we'd known each other for years. I had a few orgasms before he came. It was intimate and raw. I felt like I could be vulnerable with him.

Alessandro had turned out to be a great guide, an expert at more than just the local landscape.

Guise of Generosity

"I can give you girls a drive back to the train station," Luke offered generously. We were heading back to Sydney and had told one of the fellow travellers at the hostel. He'd been friendly with us the past few days, stopping by our room to say hi and striking up conversation when we crossed paths in the halls. Anna and I accepted his offer of a ride, since it would save us money, and we didn't want to take public transportation with all of our luggage.

When it was time to go, we lugged our things out to Luke's car in the parking lot. I'd texted Alessandro letting him know that we were leaving, and he told me he wanted to stop by the hostel to say goodbye.

I saw his tall figure as we were packing up, walking towards me. He whispered in my ear as he picked me up into a bear hug. "Bye, babe. It was amazing to meet you. Have a safe trip back to Sydney."

I was sad to be leaving him, but that's the nature of travelling. If you're lucky, you meet amazing people and experience memorable times, and then you move on. I had suspicions that I'd be back in Canberra again anyways, and could reach out then.

I walked back to Luke's car, and as Anna and I sat down he asked, "Who was that?" in a sharp tone I hadn't heard from him before.

"Oh, a friend I made here," I replied.

"You fuck him, huh?" he said. "I just saw you walking over with your booty bouncin' in those shorts." I was instantly disgusted. I was wearing a one-piece romper, which might as well have been purchased from Gap Kids. Not for the size — because it wasn't particularly small or tight, in fact it was baggy — but because it was covered in childish zigzags in blue, purple, and white. . The rest of the drive was tense. I just wanted Luke to drop us off so we could leave his car. I didn't feel safe anymore, as I realized his nice guy charade was entirely fabricated. The generosity of driving us felt more like a trap.

All Aboard!

The cruise was set to depart from the Sydney Harbour, and would stop at the Isle of Pines, Lifou, Noumea, and finally the ultimate destination, New Caledonia.

Anna and I had already packed and were going to pick up a few last-minute items before boarding in the early afternoon. We walked to a local drugstore near our hostel and, after perusing for a bit, each picked out a number of items. I had hair elastics and a new pair of sunnies.

"Feeling like pizza for lunch?" Anna ventured, knowing full well that I'd never turn down pizza. "There's a place right around the corner that's supposed to be amazing."

I nodded my head eagerly, salivating at the thought of a delicious meal and a drink in the sunshine. It was barely noon, and the heat was already becoming unbearable. We paid for our new things as if we had all the money in the world, and made our way towards the restaurant with an additional bounce in our step. No worries of work or money for the next week. A full seven days. How glorious.

"Inside or outside?" the server asked us.

"Outside!" we both proclaimed at the same time, chuckling at how we'd seemed to become one over these past few months together. Anna told me that her dad had even commented that she spoke similarly to me when they'd Skyped one time. She picked up phrases from others far more than I did, like a human sponge.

We took a seat at a high circular table outside, eyeing up the drink menu. "I'm deciding between beer and cider," I mused to Anna. "They both sound so refreshing right now."

"Oh, yeah. I'm for sure going for a cider," she agreed. I ordered a margherita pizza for myself, and Anna got a vegan pizza. I noted how drastically my eating habits had changed throughout our travels; I usually opted for frequent small meals throughout the day and would never have imagined sitting down to a full pizza by myself. Over the course of the past few months, however, with my wonky schedule, I now ate massive amounts of food a couple of times a day. I'd begun to pack on the pounds. My stomach was in a perpetual state of bloating, which I attributed to both my eating habits and the inhuman amounts of alcohol I regularly consumed.

Since arriving in Australia, Anna and I had wavered between two extremes: the stress of having no money, and the sudden accumulation of money. As I washed down my pizza with my drink, I thought about how this cruise was going to give my body and mind a much needed break somewhere in between.

The ship was smaller than the ones I'd seen in movies, and the average age of those on board was roughly sixty. I realized I truly had no excuse to drink, not with such mature shipmates.

Anna and I found our room on the inside of the ship, without any windows leading to an ocean view. Our tiny washroom was to the right as we entered, and a closet on the left. There was a small countertop and mirror to one side and finally two small separate beds, one in either corner. After dinner we took to our respective beds, each deciding to take a pill in the hopes it would help us sleep. We were also both feeling like a cold was coming on, and hoped this would help with the sore throat and congestion.

I awoke hours later in a daze to see a small man near our door, making his way from the bathroom towards us. I lifted my head, and I'm sure my face revealed my horror and confusion even in the darkness.

"I'll come back tomorrow to fix the toilet," he said, and backed out of the room.

"Anna!" I shrieked in horror.

She was a far deeper sleeper than I was, but rolled over to reply, "What?"

"Who the fuck was that?!" I was petrified, unable to move and barely sure of what had happened.

"Huh? Was someone here? I thought I heard something," she replied, turning over and allowing slumber to take her into its warm embrace again.

I was far less sleepy at this point, and sat paralyzed in fear for what felt like hours. I finally made my way into the bathroom where I stared at my own reflection, replaying what had just happened in my mind. There couldn't have actually been a man in our room, I thought, be rational. How would he have gotten in? Does he work for the cruise line? We took medication that stated plainly on the container that it may make you drowsy, that's all this is. A hallucination of sorts. A bad dream.

And so, I went back to bed.

Man of My Dreams

"Would someone have been able to get access to our room?" Anna asked the security guard a few nights later. I'd tried my best to forget about the incident, but as it turned out, it wasn't something I could easily erase from my mind.

"No, no one should be going in at that hour. You said he was there to fix the toilet?"

"Well, our toilet was broken, but we hadn't contacted anyone about it…" The intruder's mention of our toilet had served as a plausible excuse, but still didn't answer our questions; someone had either come to fix our toilet, or had used that as an excuse for being in our room to steal money from us. Either way, it was creepy.

"I can check the security footage," he reassured us, promising that if he found any suspicious activity from the first night on the cruise, he'd be sure to let us know.

Beautiful Girls

Anna and I were on the elevator, headed out to the pool deck at the back of the ship.

As the elevator stopped, an elderly couple stepped in to join us. We all stood in silence until the ding of the elevator announced that we'd reached our level. Before getting out the woman commented, "You're beautiful girls!" I smiled politely and thanked her, thinking nothing of it.

Anna, on the other hand, was put off. "Why would she say that? What does it matter what we look like? Why is our society so obsessed with looks?"

I hadn't been expecting this reaction at all. It came out of nowhere. It seemed to me that you can't be mad at an innocent grandma giving you a compliment while also earning money off of your appearance. You have to choose. It was too ironic for me to even think of a response. How could I voice this in a coherent way when she wasn't making any sense at all? Couldn't she see that she was getting naked in front of hordes of people on a daily basis? How was that okay, but one woman's harmless compliment was not?

"She didn't mean anything by it. Let's splurge and get a drink." We walked to the pool deck, where there was nothing around us but a blanket of ocean and sky. It made me realize how small I really was. It was terrifying and comforting at the same time.

"Did you see anything on the security footage?" Anna and I eagerly asked the security man, the one who'd promised us he'd look into it.

He shook his head before answering. "Nothing, and I watched the footage of your hallway for that whole night." I felt disappointed, but also relieved. I didn't want him to find anything, but it seemed almost worse this way. I felt like a fraud or a liar. I felt like I'd fabricated a story for attention. Worst of all, I felt like I couldn't trust myself anymore. Like I'd lost the ability to decipher what was real in the world.

Botox Party

"Hey, the itinerary says free champagne if we go to this Botox party!" I read aloud to Anna as we sat on our beds. We'd been taking afternoon naps the entire week on the cruise — turns out the combination of sunshine and a completely free schedule on vacation took a lot out of you.

"Botox?" She was skeptical. "I don't want to pay for that."

"It says that we don't need to pay or commit to getting anything done," I continued, trying my best to appease her. "I've heard a lot about preventative Botox. I don't want it now, necessarily, but maybe in the near future. I'd just like to get more info on it."

"Hm, alright. Let's do that, then watch the movie after dinner," she agreed.

When we walked into the information session, a few things immediately became apparent: there weren't as many people there as I thought there would be, and we were the youngest people there. By a lot.

"Well, ladies, you're all here for the Botox party?" asked a blonde lady in a white medical jacket and a full face of makeup. Everyone nodded in response.

"Okay, first thing's first — everyone please take a glass of champagne! It's probably what brought you out, after all!" she chuckled at herself. I smiled and took my flute, sipping it eagerly to ease the discomfort of having come.

The nurse introduced herself and asked us what questions we all had for her. Two ladies in their sixties wanted to know about the cost and longevity of the injections. The nurse essentially told them that each individual is different, and that we metabolize Botox differently and at different speeds. The ladies then finished their drinks and left.

Next, she turned to the other two ladies that had come together, who were easily in their eighties. They asked about Botox for some of their sagging skin, pointing to their under-eyes and tugging at their jaws. The nurse lady told them that it was too late for them to turn to Botox. They simply wouldn't get the results they wanted. They'd need a more invasive procedure, like a facelift, to see results. The ladies seemed disappointed, and left.

Finally, she turned to Anna and me and asked us why we'd come, saying we were too young. I made my point about preventative Botox, saying I'd heard about it and was curious. She told us that the youngest patient she'd ever injected was in her early twenties and had lived in Hawaii her entire life. Apparently she'd been a sun worshiper who had never worn sunscreen. As a result, she'd developed premature lines in her forehead, which Botox had helped.

I left the event thinking about the other women who'd attended the Botox party, especially the women in their eighties who had lived such full lives. Why did they care about the lines on their faces, the evidence of laughter and joy? The marks etched into their skin where the sun had warmed it? Would that be me at sixty or even eighty? Was that me now?

Luck of the Draw

While we were on the cruise, we had spotty internet access that allowed us to stay connected to our lives on the mainland. Through Facebook, we found out that the Travel Trio were planning to do their month-long excursion along the East Coast in a few weeks. We also found out that they had so many backpackers interested in joining them that they were drawing names from a hat. It was a nerve-wracking time as Anna and I hunched over our laptop, listening to each name being read aloud. Miraculously, we heard each of our names included on the list. Hallelujah! The trip was a go.

Tease Gentlemen's Club

We still had a few weeks before our first real backpacking adventure in Australia, and I was beyond stoked. The reality, though, was that we needed money.

"I'm gonna to look into working somewhere else," I thought aloud as Anna and I unpacked our things. We were back at the Zing Backpackers hostel in Kings Cross, and I was happy to know that this time we were only staying for three weeks before leaving Sydney for good. We'd gotten our private room again at the hostel, but had plans to travel to Cairns with other young people (as the Travel Trio had made it clear they were only accepting people under the age of thirty).

"Okay, that makes sense, since you hated it so much at Diamond Dolls by the end," Anna replied. "I don't like Strippers, either, but I make good money, so I'll just put up with it for a few more weeks." That was that.

I pulled out the card I'd received on our first night in Sydney when we'd visited a few different strip clubs, this one from the place across the street from Strippers where I'd seen the girl dancing with the faux fur while fully exposed. The place was called Tease, and the name on the card read Jimmy. I pulled out my cell and hoped for the best.

I started that night.

I walked into the club with my own drinks in hand, and after descending the dark staircase, I headed straight to the bar. One of the most striking differences between Diamond Dolls and Tease was the bar; Tease served only beer, with no liquor options. Girls were expected to bring our own alcohol if we wanted to drink. There were two large fridges with glass doors, similar to a vending machine. I placed my mixed drinks in the fridge, making sure to take one and crack it open before making my way towards the dressing room.

Another difference was the expectation that we get fully naked while on stage. Customers could purchase "tipping vouchers," which were just little paper cards that the club had made for tipping if they preferred that to cash. They could then put it in a girl's costume more times because each one was worth a very small amount.

The dressing room was similar to the other ones I'd seen: a long room with mirrors and lights the length of one wall. There were lockers for valuables, too — a nice added touch, I thought.

I changed into my outfit, my black bra and underwear with little pink bows. I had decided to add knee length black socks to the ensemble to make myself look slightly more edgy. As I exited, I noted that the private dance rooms were tiny, allowing only one or two dancers in at a time. They closed with black curtains that slid across a metal bar.

"There are rooms upstairs for when someone books a longer time slot, like an hour or more," Jimmy, the short manager, had explained to me. He was giving me a quick tour of the club before my shift began, and the club would presumably get busier. He had grey hair and wore a t-shirt and plaid shorts. I wasn't sure what to make of him just yet. "You'll have to go outside to get up there," he explained, leading the way. I followed him outside and up a flight of stairs to what I presumed was the VIP section. There were a handful of rooms with couches and tables, along with a number of other furnishings. It felt far more like an old house than an extension of a strip club.

When it was my turn to go on stage, I felt slightly apprehensive about getting completely bare-ass-naked with the stage so close to the front row. It turns out, though, that you can overcome this fear by getting super drunk.

"Can I get a dance?" a young guy with dark hair, tattoos, and a nose ring asked me.

"Of course!" I took his hand and led him to a private room.

"You're pretty badass," he told me while I was grinding on top of him, "with your septum ring and black outfit." Huh. I'd been called many things, but people usually said that I looked innocent rather than badass. I thought of one of the dancers at Diamond Dolls who was really thin, had long black hair, and was covered in tattoos — including an awesome neck piece which I can only imagine hurt like a bitch. She went by the name Jekyll, which a customer once joked about, saying to me that her persona was pretty forthright. Now, Jeykll was a badass. Me? Not so much. But I could own it in the moment. It's fun pretending to be something you're not.

Second Floor VIP

One insanely drunk night at the club, Jimmy asked me to dance for him in the VIP room. I'd never had a manager ask for a dance, and didn't think I had the option of turning down the request. We went to one of the rooms upstairs, and he carried a black old-school boombox with him for music. I gave him a dance on the couch. We chatted for a bit, and then he gave me the money. I didn't know if I was supposed to give the dance "on the house," so I was happy to get paid.

The night progressed as usual.

At the end of my shift, Jimmy asked me to stay behind to chat. I obliged, hoping I wasn't in trouble for anything, since I wanted to maximize my income before taking off more than a month to travel.

"In here, Amber," Jimmy pointed towards a private room to the side. Everyone had already cleared out, including security who worked the door. I was so out of it that I followed his instructions.

"Dance for me," he ordered. So I did.

The next thing I knew, Jimmy had his hand on my vagina. Then he stood up and pulled his penis out, shoving it into my mouth. I could have bitten it. I could have run away. I didn't, though, because I could barely process what was going on. So I began giving him head, until my brain began to comprehend that I didn't want this after all. I didn't want to give him oral sex, and I hadn't done anything to lead him on. I got up and stuttered something about needing to leave.

For the rest of the nights that I worked there, I handled my anxiety by pre-drinking harder than I had ever drunk in my life. I brought more than a six-pack of drinks for my shift, too.

Fly on the Wall

"Jimmy's in a horrible mood tonight, eh," one of the dancers voiced to the rest of us who were seated around a high top bar table.

"One night he went off on me and threw a speaker at my head," another girl shared, clearly still shocked at the incident.

"He's fuckin' insane." The first girl shook her head in disbelief.

It was a strange thing, listening in. I felt like a fly on the wall; I was allowed to hear my coworkers thoughts, but I rarely reciprocated with my own. In this case, I chose not to share my own experiences with Jimmy. I wasn't even sure how I could explain our relationship.

The conversation took a turn, and the girls began talking about other clubs in Kings Cross. "Oh, there's that place across the street literally just called Strippers, where the girls are all sleeping with customers," a dancer said.

"Oh, yeah, that's a brothel, not a strip club," another girl said, and the others chuckled along.

"My friend works there," I finally chimed in. "I think she just dances, though." I suddenly felt unsure of Anna's nightly shifts. Strippers stayed open far later than either of my clubs had in Sydney, and I thought back to the bedrooms I'd seen upstairs.

"Honey, if your friend is working there, she's giving more than lap dances," the first dancer said, looking into my eyes. "She's giving extras."

I didn't say anything else, just thought about how much alcohol Anna and I were both consuming before work. I thought about how her one bottle of wine before her shift began increasing, and how she'd now been taking another one for the night. I thought how she'd been making far more money than I had at Diamond Dolls, which was the most upscale club in the area. I thought about how little we discussed our work experiences during the day, because we each wanted to forget and escape.

Casino

I sat chatting with a customer when I noticed Jimmy talking to a middle-aged man. Something led me to believe they knew one another. The man made his way over to me and asked me for a dance upstairs in the VIP room.

Upstairs, we took a seat in the room that I'd been in before with Jimmy. The man's name was Nate. He told me he worked for a large tech company, and made a lot of money. I don't know why men who are paying for female companionship feel the need to impress. He complimented me, saying he knew Shania Twain and that she had soft skin; of course, he said,t my skin was "even softer." Nate offered me a line of blow, which he cut neatly on the end table. After watching him do a line, I happily accepted.

"In university, I founded a startup," he said. "I guess that was the beginning of my business career." He told me about his business, which was essentially a brothel. He hired female students who were willing to sleep with guys for money and pimped them out. "Everyone wanted to do it," he assured me. "I had some girls coming asking me for work once they found out a friend did it. That's how we grew. I hired a couple buddies and we made sure the girls were safe, even began working out of a building I rented." He took a swig of his beer and snorted another line.

"Oh, wow, that's insane," I replied, eager to hear more, but also perturbed. I knew firsthand that girls that age were capable of getting themselves in over their heads. I could see them thinking the money would be easy, with just a little time invested in work for fairly big payouts. I'm sure some of them thought they could handle it, that it was only a physical act. But I don't think we always know how things impact us down the road. We don't know how deeply the physical and emotional are interconnected.

I didn't say much in our hour and a half in that room. I didn't have to: Nate was perfectly content to keep talking.

"Well, I wanna keep partying," he ventured. "Wanna hit up the casino after this?"

Why the hell not? I thought to myself. I wouldn't be sleeping anytime soon anyways with the combination of booze and cocaine coursing through my veins.

"Sure," I shrugged. "I'll have to change into better clothes than what I came in, though."

We agreed to take a cab back to my hostel, where I'd change and grab whatever I needed and then head to the casino from there.

Casinos never sleep. The fluorescent lights shine bright at all hours, confusing all those inside as to the time of day. The bright flashing colours, the whirs of the machines — everything is created to entice us to play. The first time I stepped inside a casino I was overloaded.

I followed Nate up a set of stairs and into a wing of the casino with an assortment of slot machines. We sat down, and he put in a couple hundred dollars and began pressing buttons. A waiter came around to us: "Drinks?"

"Rum and cokes, please," Nate ordered, barely taking his eyes off the machine.

With each press of the button he was losing money, until he suddenly won a few hundred dollars. He pressed a button and cashed out. "Let's move to this one." He pointed to a different machine, and I obliged, admitting that I knew nothing about slots and thought everyone inevitably lost on them. To me, it seemed that people were always in a trance with them, mindlessly pressing buttons.

We chatted a bit, and he offered me some more blow. "I'll pass you my drink, and it will be at the bottom," Nate explained. "Just take it to the bathroom."

I did as instructed, walking in my booty heels and black high-waisted skirt to the women's bathroom and locking myself in a stall. This was the first time in my life I had cut my own line, and the first time I'd ever done cocaine alone. I snorted the blow and walked out in a confident beeline to Nate, who appeared to be winning more money on this slot. I handed him the drink and baggy back. "Here, take this," he said, handing me the winnings of the game.

"Are you sure?" I asked, slightly uneasy. He nodded with a smile on his face. "Okay, thanks!" The night continued with Nate winning money and both of us taking turns in the bathroom.

The casino was large and mostly deserted. On one trip to the bathroom, I heard security yelling at a girl to get out of her stall and leave. She seemed to be very intoxicated, bordering on passing out. I waited until I heard them all leave before snorting a line.

"Let's go to my hotel. I'm right across the street," Nate suggested, making more of a statement than a question. Very conveniently located, I thought to myself. Something he'd failed to mention when we were at the club. I don't know whether it was the hundreds of dollars I had in my clutch or the fact that I was now even more out of it than when we'd arrived, but I decided to go with him.

We walked into the marble foyer of the hotel, and I suddenly became acutely aware of how this looked. There was security at the entrance, and I was a twenty-three-year-old following a wealthy middle-aged man to his hotel room. I was wearing heavy stripper makeup and tight clothes, and my heels clacked on the hard floor as I followed him to the elevator.

"There's toothpaste in the bathroom if you wanna freshen up," Nate said, ever the gentleman.

"Okay, thanks." I scurried into the bathroom and locked the door, looking at myself in the mirror. I took some toothpaste onto my finger and did a poor job of "freshening up," then joined Nate on the bed. He leaned in and started kissing me. To my surprise, it was nice. I kissed him back. He began undressing me, pulling me down as he made his way down to my vagina and started performing oral. I let him. His stubble felt nice. I let him continue until I orgasmed, then suddenly felt sober and realized I didn't want him inside me.

Thankfully, Nate was a good guy. I told him to stop, and he listened. I had an overwhelming sense that this was all wrong. I felt cheap. I don't know why I didn't feel cheap while he was eating me out, but I knew I didn't want to return the favour, and so I got dressed and left.

Looking back on it and counting my money in the hostel room, I realized that I may have used Nate more than he used me.

West Coast Trippin'

Anna and I were packed and ready to go: out of Sydney, and out of Kings Cross for good.

We met all of our traveling companions that morning, as we boarded the big white bus that we'd be taking with the Travel Trio from Sydney to Cairns. There were fourteen of us in total: Anna and myself, the Canadians; two French travelers, Eric and Aris, who'd come separately; two guys from Texas, Mike and Josh; another American girl, Kristen; two British travelers, Emma and Ron; two German girls, Mia and Johanna; and of course the three Aussies who were running the tour — Blake, his twin brother Jack, and Seth.

They'd printed off a photo they'd found on each of our Facebook profiles and plastered them onto the window of the bus. It made me feel like a part of the group before we even knew one another. We all introduced ourselves and hopped on the bus.

"Where's Mike?" one of the Aussies asked Josh, who I later found out was travelling with his brother.

"He was out late last night. He'll be here soon," Josh answered. I was surprised he didn't have a Southern accent. We waited around for

Exposed

a bit, and finally a guy with dark facial hair and sporty sunglasses — Mike — sauntered onto the bus and took a seat on the floor. He put his hood up and laid down in the aisle, taking a snooze while the rest of us got to know one another a bit.

At some point Mike resurrected himself, and suddenly he and Josh were at the back of the bus, pouring goon for everyone in plastic cups. This time the goon was just cheap, shitty white wine from a box, rather than the mixed concoction I'd previously tasted at Peter Pan's Travel Adventures.

"Want some?" They looked at me. I couldn't very well turn down the first drink of the trip! I had worked the night before, but had left the club before 2 am so that I wouldn't be too exhausted.

"Sure," I said, taking the cup. We all cheersed to an amazing trip ahead of us and took a sip, hoping for the best.

Later in the day we all got off for a bathroom break. As we boarded the bus to continue to Byron Bay, I looked at where I'd been sitting before, and saw that everyone had rearranged. I guess it was obvious that I wasn't sure where to go, because Jack, one of the Aussies sitting near the front, pointed to the one vacant spot. "There's a seat beside Mike," he announced. Mike hadn't boarded yet, so I figured that if he wanted to sit with his buddy he could choose to. I took a seat.

"Hey, what's your name again?" Mike asked moments later as he sat down beside me. We began chatting. I found out that he was thirty, and that he had broken up with his long-term girlfriend recently before deciding to travel with his friend. He didn't want anything to hold him back from new experiences. By the end of the day, I was laughing hysterically. I had seriously misjudged him. He was hilarious and kind. "I love your laugh," he said, and chuckled along with me every time.

Byron Bay

We drove that first day for over thirteen hours, finally making it to our first destination. "We're stopping at the bottle shop for anyone who wants to pick up alcohol!" Seth announced.

We were camping for two nights in Byron. Our campsite was right beside the beach, just walking distance to local shops. The tour guides were kind enough to provide us with tents, pillows, and sleeping bags; all that was required of us was to pay the fee to stay there.

Anna and I had purchased a large bottle of vodka on our cruise, since they sold things duty-free. We brought it out and shared it with our travel companions, deeming this occasion worthy of cracking into the big bottle. The group went out drinking together that first night, walking around the cute coastal town of Byron and getting to know one another.

"So who is everyone into?" Kristen asked the girls, who had clumped together, talking. Ron was also with us, and shared that sadly, none of the guys were his type. "I'm kind of into Jack," Kristen shared, sighing like a schoolgirl at the thought of him. "And we all know who you're into," she added, looking me squarely in the face. The others nodded along. I'd had a good time talking with Mike on the drive, but I didn't know that everyone had noticed us conversing. I had assumed everyone else was just as immersed in their own chats.

At the end of the night, we all found our tents and slept soundly.

It was the first and last time I shared a tent with Anna.

The next afternoon, we were all sitting on the beach chatting and looking out at the ocean. Anna and I wanted to get a blanket and sweater from our bags. We walked to our tent and crossed paths with Jack.

"Be careful," he said. "Last time I was here, there was a huge python right along there." He pointed to the chain link fence right beside our campsite. I paused for a second, taking in his expression and tone to try to gauge if he was being serious.

"Oh my god," I said, suddenly nervous for our safety.

"He's clearly joking." Anna smirked at me, as if the joke went right over my head.

"Nah, I'm not," Jack replied, straight-faced. He turned down the path to the beach, and we watched our footing as we gathered our things and followed him.

Brisbane

After the first night, I found Mike's tent and we became inseparable. He felt like home. He quickly became my best friend on the trip. The dynamics of having others with us gave Anna and me a nice break from being glued to one another.

In Brisbane, we were staying at a hostel called Big Bird Backpackers. The French girl, Aris, had begun seeing the other Texan, Josh. Since there were fourteen of us, we split up, and the four of us who were "coupled up" took a room together.

We spent the day walking around the city center, and took a cruise down the river on a boat. That night, we all went out to a few different bars. Mike and I decided to go back to the hostel before everyone else, hoping to have a moment to ourselves. "Big Bird Backpackers, please," we said to the taxi driver. The driver paused for a moment. Mike asked, "Do you know where that is?"

The man nodded — "Oh, yes, yes," he said — and began driving.

He stopped at a big building, saying that we just had to walk around it to get to the hostel. We paid him and left, making our way inside the large building. We quickly realized that we were nowhere near the hostel. I don't know if language had been a barrier in this exchange, but based on the cab driver's initial pause, I concluded that he just didn't know where the hostel was and didn't want to lose the money.

Mike and I walked around for hours, stopping at a corner store to buy chips when I got hungry. We finally made it to our hostel in the early hours of the morning. So much for our alone time.

Fraser Island

One of the greatest things about the East Coast trip was that while we split gas money, we paid our own way for hostels and campsites, and got to choose whether we wanted to pay for any extra activities. Those of us who opted to pay the additional fees for a night on Fraser Island were getting ready to leave the mainland, where the rest of our friends were going to be camping to save money.

We took a ferry to the island. When we got there, we all boarded a tour bus. It felt like we were on water rather than sandy roads as the bus bounded from side to side, up and down. If it hadn't been a guided tour, I'm not sure I would have remained so calm.

"If anyone wants to get up early tomorrow, the sunrise is at about 5:30 a.m.," one of the guides said. "If you walk from the hostel down to the beach, it's really worth your while." I thought to myself that a sunrise would be nice to see. I'd seen dozens of stunning sunsets on different beaches of Australia, and each one seemed to give me a renewed outlook on life, but I had yet to see more than a couple sunrises.

In the morning, I heard some of my friends shuffling around while I laid in bed. I looked up to see Emma put some sweatpants on and run out the door. Still groggy, I rolled over and closed my eyes again. *But I'm already up...* I thought. I rolled back over and opened my eyes to see that Ron was now awake as well.

"Wanna go?" he asked me, clearly also questioning whether forcing himself up would be worthwhile at this ungodly hour. I nodded, took a deep breath, and jumped out of bed. We ran after Emma, reaching the beach just in time to watch the sun begin to rise over the horizon. The sky was warm, with different yellows, oranges, pinks, and reds reflected on the ocean's surface.

I stood there silently until the sun was overhead, then turned to Ron. "That was definitely worth getting up for," I said. He agreed.

Yeppoon

"Anyone who wants to hop on the bus to get back to camp, we'll meet back here at 4:00 p.m.," Jack informed everyone before we got off the bus. "That way we can get back and make dinner at the campsite. Anyone who wants the exercise can feel free to walk the length of the beach, which leads straight back to our campsite."

We all spent the afternoon in the town of Yeppoon, browsing shops and getting food. Anna and I mostly just explored, managing to save most of our money and splurging only on a nice lunch. Food was something we never skimped on.

As the afternoon progressed, the sun shone on us and I felt like walking might do me some good. "How do you feel about walking instead of taking the bus?" I asked Anna.

"Hmm... If you want to, I'm down," she agreed. "We'll probably be some of the only ones walking."

The beach was right next to the city center; we walked and chatted as the ocean lapped at the shore. My mindset had drastically changed over the past couple of weeks of traveling. Anna and I had both formed solid friendships with our traveling companions, and we were happy to be away from the clubs.

"Look at the sand here," Anna pointed down to thousands of tiny balls of sand, neatly compacted by the crabs. We'd both been walking without our sandals for a while, and I could feel the hard balls underneath my feet. It was fascinating to see how such tiny creatures could alter the entire beach.

As we continued walking, it dawned on us that we had no idea how close we were to the campsite. We also hadn't paid any attention to the actual name of the site, since we relied on our friends at all times.

"The sun is starting to set," I remarked, worry beginning to creep into my mind. The temperature was dropping.

"Okay, we could have passed it. Maybe we should ask someone," Anna said. But when we looked around, we realized that we hadn't passed anyone on the beach for a long while.

"Honestly, I'm getting kinda nervous," I said, realizing how little time we'd have to get off the beach and to our campsite before the sun set. Animals would start moving around soon, and we didn't have anything to keep us safe. We also had no idea how far we were from the campsite, or which direction we were supposed to be heading in.

"Yeah, maybe we should head that way towards a road," Anna suggested, pointing away from the ocean. When we'd first set out walking, the landscape had been flat, but now when I looked where she'd pointed I saw that there were rolling hills and sand dunes. We tried climbing them, but found it too hard. We'd have to keep walking to a flatter area with less brush in the way.

We continued on, shivering.

"Look!" I pointed to a smaller sand dune." Let's try again.". We managed to climb over to a walkway, where we came across two teenage girls walking a dog on a leash.

"Excuse me," gasped Anna, "would you happen to know where the nearest campsite is?"

"Umm… There aren't any nearby," said the girl holding the leash. "The nearest one is over five miles that way." She pointed in the direction of town.

"Oh my god, we went way too far," Anna replied, staring at me. "Thanks so much!" The girls looked curiously at one another and continued on their evening stroll.

We walked and walked until we found a main road that ran parallel to the beach, ensuring that we were headed in the right direction this time. When we finally got to the campsite, we each made a beeline for the bathroom, examining our windswept hair, exhilarated to be back safely. At this point we were joking about how the others would react. Of course it had to be the two Canadian girls, who always seemed to struggle with the simplest tasks.

When we got near the tents, we found everyone eating dinner under a covered communal cooking area. They didn't even seem to notice we'd been missing.

Airlie Beach and Whitsunday

My feet got absolutely destroyed from the incident on the beach. All those hours of walking had left behind leathery calluses covering both of my soles. I still wore my flip flops around, but it took a few days to recover.

We were now stopped in Airlie Beach, where we'd be spending a couple of nights at a hostel. The group wanted to do a day tour to see Whitsunday Island, which included visiting the world-renowned swirling sands of Whitehaven and snorkeling around the Great Barrier Reef. Mike and Josh were sitting this one out because they were getting concerned about finances — a fair concern, considering they'd worked for a few months in Sydney for a friend's startup and had yet to see a paycheque.

The rest of us were up early and ready for the day. We walked down to the waterfront and hopped onto the tour boat.

Our first stop on the island was Whitehaven Beach. The weather wasn't on our side, unfortunately, and it drizzled on us as we walked around and learned that the sand was made almost entirely of silica, that it was unusually soft to the touch, and that it was illegal for us to take any with us when we left. I hadn't considered taking sand as a keepsake, but now that the tour guides had put that idea in my head, it took all my self-restraint not to fill my pockets.

After boarding the boat again, we were alerted to the presence of a circling tiger shark. "That's a big boy!" one of the guides told us. "They're one of the most dangerous sharks for humans; they'll eat just about anythin'!" Away we went towards our next destination: snorkeling. Oh, how fun, I thought to myself. Can't wait to hop into the water now.

"Ladies and gentlemen," the same tour guide announced, addressing us all on a loudspeaker, "we are about to enter an area of water that we call the Toilet Bowl. You'll see why in a minute!" Sure enough, the entire boat began thrashing about in the waves, until it felt like we were about to capsize. Anna began screaming and pulled out a shawl from her bag. I looked at her with equal amounts of terror, but I remained silent. She handed me the shawl and we hid beneath it, as if hiding our eyes from our reality would change it.

As the ocean waves calmed, we came to a stop near a small island, around which we were told there were lots of colorful coral and fish species. We all jumped out of the boat and began swimming around with our snorkels and flippers on. I was absolutely amazed at how much was going on beneath the surface of the ocean. The way the light hit the water and illuminated everything made me feel like I was in The Little Mermaid. I had to remind myself that it wasn't a fairytale.

Maggie Island

"We're going to a place called Magnetic Island," Seth informed the group as we left Airlie Beach. "It's right across from Townsville," he explained. That meant very little to me. All I knew was that it was north of where we'd just been, and we'd have to take a ferry to get over to it from the mainland.

By the time we got across and set up our tents at the campsite, I was exhausted and made the call — for once — to get to bed early.

When I arose in the morning, I was overcome with the beauty of the place. It felt tropical, with large boulders lining the turquoise water. During our short stay, I'd spend many hours perched atop the boulders listening to music with Ron and Emma, learning about the true meaning behind each song; Emma was a bit of a music connoisseur.

"Why's there a pool when we're right on the ocean?" I asked the Aussies we were travelling with.

"You can't go swimming here this time of year, because of the box jellyfish," Blake replied solemnly. He didn't expand on the subject at all, so later in the day I brought it up to Mike.

"Oh, they're a really dangerous type of jellyfish," he said. "Apparently they've killed people before. Their venom can paralyze you or put you into cardiac arrest."

Later that day, Mike and I found ourselves on the beach covered in sand, and we each ran into the water to clean off. I didn't see anyone else do that. It's possible I have a death wish, I thought.

Cairns

Anna, Mike, Josh, Aris, and I were staying in a hostel down the street from where the rest of our group was staying. Ourst was about seven dollars less every night. Unfortunately, Mike and Josh still hadn't been paid by their friend; this had become a tense topic for the Texans. Anna and I had given them a couple hundred dollars to tide them over until the end of the trip, since we'd noticed that they'd started prioritizing nights out and alcohol over good meals due to their lack of funds. My gift to our friends was sorely missed, however, when I looked at my bank account and came to the realization that I'd have to go back to work immediately after our trip.

"Look up," Mike said one evening as the sun was setting. The two of us laid near the outdoor pool at our hostel in the grass, staring at the sky. There were swarms of thousands of small dark birds flying above us.

"Wait…" I said, looking closer. "Are those… bats?!" I asked Mike.

"Yeah! I read on a sign in town that they're fruit bats, and they move at dawn and dusk to eat." He gazed up with a smile on his face, transfixed at the sight.

Daintree Rainforest

"They haven't found a body yet," Seth said to those of us listening as we drove down a steep road in the Daintree Rainforest, north of Cairns.

"And they won't," said the young male hitchhiker we'd picked up, a local who was coming back to the area from a mini vacation. "The crocs will put it under a rock, and when the body decomposes, they'll eat the fish that come to feast." There was no emotion in the man's voice. His matter-of-factness about something so recent and tragic scared me a bit. I looked out the window at the yellow caution tape surrounding an area of beach, with numerous police vehicles parked to the side.

We were on an excursion for the day, where we'd planned to explore the rainforest and walking some trails. A woman had gone missing the night before, after we'd already planned to come on our day trip.

According to the news, she'd been wading into the water with a friend when she'd suddenly been pulled under. Her friend had tried to help, but there was no hope.

"What are these signs?" I pointed to a yellow sign on the side of the road that just had a picture of what looked like Big Bird. No words were written; it was expected that we knew what the message was.

"That's to let us know of cassowaries nearby," the hitchhiker answered. "They're huge birds that can do some damage if they kick ya," he said. I started wondering why we'd come to the rainforest.

"I saw this on the Nature Channel," Mike explained. He began slapping the surface of the water with a stick he'd found, creating ripples that spread in circular rings, getting larger and larger until they disappeared. "The crocs can feel the change in the water and think it's an animal. That's when they strike," he continued. I stared at the water, mesmerized by the rings and the power of nature.

"Everyone get away from the water!" one of the Aussies yelled to us. "And make sure you don't turn your back to it. You need to see if something comes out," he warned, clearly on edge. Mike stopped slapping the water, no longer laughing at the action, with the grim realization that nature could be ruthless.

Goodbyes

It was my twenty-fourth birthday, and the night before we would all go our own ways. It was bittersweet. I was grateful to have met everyone and gotten the experience of sightseeing with new friends; it was an experience I'd cherish for the rest of my life. But Anna and I could only ignore the numbers in our bank accounts for so long. It was time to get back to work immediately. We didn't have enough money to last more than a week in a hostel.

"Want to go to Brisbane? I liked it there, and would love to explore the city more," Anna asked. "I looked it up, and there's a club walking distance to a few hostels right in the CBD," she continued, proving that this was something she'd put some thought into.

I thought back to the night when Mike and I got lost trying to find our way back to the Big Bird Backpackers. I was overcome with sadness; we hadn't even said our goodbyes to the group yet, and I already felt empty and alone. I loved Mike. I loved our group. I didn't love stripping, and it was beginning to feel like it wasn't worth it anymore. I want to see as much of the country as I can, but I'm not going to continue on to New Zealand, I decided. Anna and a few of the others we travelled with had already decided they'd continue onto the nearby islands once their year was up in Australia. As much as I wanted to join them, the toll that dancing was taking on me was too much. It didn't feel worth it anymore.

"I really liked Brisbane," I agreed. We bought our plane tickets that day.

It was the morning of everyone's departure. The bus and the Aussies were heading back down the coast to Sydney. They would be taking the Texans with them and dropping them off in Townsville, across from Magnetic Island. Our American friends had managed to secure work at the campsite where we'd stayed, which was perfect because they still hadn't seen a cent from their previous job. This way, they had a place to stay and food.

Anna and I were among the few who would be staying a couple extra days, before hopping on our flight to Brisbane to resume working in clubs. A few of the others were leaving Australia altogether — headed home, wherever that was for them.

We woke up and hugged goodbye outside our hostel, and when the bus rolled out of view down the street I felt a quiet despair. I looked over at Anna and knew that despite our own ups and downs, I was thankful we'd stuck together through this. I couldn't imagine being alone.

Dizzy & Disoriented

At some point during the East Coast trip, I must have gotten water in my left ear. I'd gone to the chemist, the Australian pharmacy, to buy some ear cleanser and drops, but to no avail. What began as an annoying feeling of water in my ear had progressed to the point where I could now barely hear anything out of that ear. In fact, when I slept on my right side the world went silent. The only time I enjoyed it was when Anna snored. When I walked around, I felt dizzy and disoriented, almost almost off-balance.

Now back in Brisbane, Anna and I had checked into a private room at our new hostel. "Wanna walk around downtown?" Anna asked. "There's a club that we can check out, it looks like it's pretty close." It was a sunny day, but despite the nice weather, we were both in low spirits. We'd gone from being with a group of people 24/7 without any real worries of finances, to being just the two of us, desperate for work.

When we arrived at the club, Brisbane's Babes, and told the bouncer we were inquiring about work, he waived the entry fee. We walked down a dark staircase into the club and went straight to the long bar. We got a tour of the club, which was quite a unique establishment. It was decorated nicely and very sleek, with a few different rooms. First, we saw the main area where the bar was located, the changerooms for strippers in the back, and one of the main stages, which was a circular moving platform. "Two girls dance on it at all times," we were informed, before heading into the other rooms. Off to the side, there was a large private dance room, its size giving me hope that it was often busy enough here to fill it up. In the very back, we came to another room with open showers and a large jacuzzi bathtub for "private spa bookings." I was intrigued, and wondered how often girls got these bookings.

"You'll need a dress or skirt to wear while you're on the floor, and a large piece of jewelry as well," the manager told us. We agreed, promising to find appropriate attire.

We were to start the next evening.

Brisbane's Babes

If I'd thought it was difficult walking around city streets without the ability to hear out of one ear, I was in for a reality check at the club. I had to make sure that clients were on the right hand side of me in order to converse. I had to do this in a way so that I didn't have to explain that I couldn't currently hear out of one ear, because I'm pretty sure that a clogged ear wouldn't sound too sexy. It was exhausting.

"I'm like the house mom here," a girl told me. "Call me Foxy." Foxy was eyeing me up in the back room where we were each giving private dances. She had dark hair and looked to be about my age

A guy who struggled to look me in the eye had bought a dance. He was very kind and warm-hearted. It felt a bit like I was stealing or taking advantage of him, because it was obvious that he had some sort of disability. I told myself that if I wasn't giving him a dance, someone else would be. At least I cared and wanted to treat him with kindness, I justified it as he handed me the cash.

Later on in the evening, I saw Foxy with a group of young guys. They asked me to join them. I sat down and we chatted for a while. Foxy left, and one of the guys told me they were on MDMA. "Have you ever done it?" he inquired.

"A couple of times," I answered honestly, "but not recently."

"Want some?" he offered.

I didn't give much thought to it. I was pretty miserable, my ear was pissing me off, and I didn't want to be there. Doing it might make this shift less shitty.

"Sure," I agreed. He told me he'd pass me a drink, and the baggy would be underneath — just like I'd done before at the Sydney casino with the baggy of coke. We were seated beside the bathroom, a choice I now realized was intentional. I took his drink and made my way to the bathroom. When I looked at the baggy I saw crystals. I'd never done MDMA in this form; it had always been in a pill I swallowed. I decided to lick my finger, dip it into the bag and rub it along my gums, the way people do the last bits of cocaine in the movies. As soon as I'd done it I tasted the most vile, bitter taste I'd ever encountered. I had no idea if I'd done too much or too little, so I did some more for good measure, and left the bathroom.

Not long afterwards, my jaw was clattering like mad, and I couldn't get it to stop. The guy who'd given me the drugs offered me some gum, which helped a little. He also bought a dance from me. We were in the private dance room and Foxy was there, watching me from the side. I imagine she knew I was on MDMA; I wondered if she was too.

I started heating up, and decided to make my way to the bar and pour myself a glass of ice water. I hoped it would sober me up some, so I kept chugging. I looked on the spinning stage to see a very curvy woman with leather accessories, including a whip and a dog collar. She seemed to be giving a show playing the role of dominatrix. I felt even more out of it.

By the time we left, I was high as hell and bloated with water. Anna and I changed and started walking back to the hostel, when I suddenly had to vomit. I looked at her quickly and then projectile vomited water all over the side of a building. It happened once more on our walk home before I began feeling better. I was still high, but at least my stomach wasn't so full.

Dark Days, Darker Nights

"Camille is going away for a couple of months and needs someone to watch the dogs and the house," Anna explained to me. We were deciding where to go next. We hadn't managed to pocket much money since the East Coast trip, and were now presented with the opportunity to go back to Melbourne with a free place to stay. It was a hard offer to turn down. Camille's house had been a safe haven, removed from the CBD. It was a bit of a trek to get to the clubs from there, but we were more than willing to commit to the transportation costs and time to save on living expenses.

Also on our minds was the fact that we were now going into Australia's winter, and would be house sitting over July and August. While I knew it wouldn't be anything like Canada's winter, I had hoped to be further North to avoid cool temperatures altogether. But a free house is a free house. What other choice did we have?

"Ron's looking to see Melbourne too," Anna continued. We had stayed in touch with several of our traveller friends

"Oh, that would be awesome. Would Camille be cool with him staying with us?" I inquired, hoping she would be. I'd learned on our trip that it was beneficial to change up the dynamics. Things were increasingly tense between the two of us, so we could use Ron as a buffer.

As it turned out, Camille wasn't okay with Ron living at her house, since she had never met him. Anna didn't care; she insisted that he come. "Ron, it's fine!" We were video chatting with him, and she maintained that Camille would be fine with it, that he should come stay with us and we'd have adventures together.

"Are you certain? I don't want to get anyone in trouble," he said, contemplating the offer. Anna hadn't made it clear that Camille had explicitly said no. Ever the gentleman, but even more frugal than the two of us, he finally conceded. "Okay, my lease ends on my room here next week. I'll look into buying a flight," he agreed.

Anna finally told the full truth after he'd moved in.

Deja Vu

Anna and I contacted the very first club we'd ever danced at, asking to come in on Friday to work. To our surprise, they agreed.

It felt strange going back there, since so much had happened. When we walked into the dressing rooms, I recognized some of the faces. Others were new. One of the blonde girls who had worked there months prior now had the addition of fake breasts adhered to her chest; something she'd talked about before I left. She'd swapped out her bleach blonde hair in favour of a less intense dirty blonde. "Now that I have the fake boobs, I felt like it was too much," she explained to the rest of us. Sofia was doing her makeup, and explaining how to do a less intense smoky eye.

"So where did you guys go?" one of the dancers asked, curious about our travels.

"We stayed in Sydney for a couple of months, and then did a month-long trip up the East Coast to Cairns," I explained. "We travelled in a bus with fourteen of us in total. It was a lot of fun!" I thought back to the trip. Describing our adventures made me nostalgic, even though my experience abroad was still ongoing.

"Yeah, it was great. We met lots of backpackers along the way and managed to do it without spending too much money," Anna chimed in.

"Wow, that's amazing," another girl added after listening in. Some of the girls asked about dancing in Sydney, voicing their desire to go there to strip. The questions brought me back to King's Cross and the underbelly of night life. I tried my best to shrug it off, and left the dressing room to head to the elevator.

The night began like any other. I did my stage performance and waited for the club to fill up. I was sitting on a stool at the back of the club when I saw him. A few guys were walking from the bar to find seats, when Alex stared me dead in the eyes. He kept walking and took a seat directly in front of the main stage. My heart skipped a beat and I had to remind myself to breathe.

"Alexander is here," I whispered, turning to Anna, "Ew, I can't believe it. Our first night back..."

"Oh my god." She took a moment to absorb the information. "I guess telling his girlfriend about you didn't change much. What do you want to do?"

I thought about it. I didn't want him to have any power over me. I was here to make money. But the longer I considered it, the more

I dreaded going on stage right in front of him. Exposing myself like that would be different when we had this history. I'd started to develop feelings for him, and he'd been lying the entire time, hiding himself while I'd been true. I felt like the sight of me dancing intimately on stage was something he no longer deserved. "Let's go," I said. Anna nodded, and we made our way to the elevator to go downstairs. When I heard the announcer introduce me to the stage, we were running out of the building.

Where Strippers Go To Die

"I was reading reviews of this club online," one of the dancers told us, "and one of them said that it's where strippers go when they've been kicked out of every other club in Melbourne. It said it's where strippers go to die." She burst out laughing. "I mean, it's true for me," she continued. "I've been kicked out of everywhere else, so I had to work here."

I didn't laugh. We were at a whole other kind of club. This wasn't the downtown core anymore. When you walked into the building, the first thing you noticed was the sheer size of the place. It was one huge room with a large stage, a laughably small bar, and dark, sticky seating. The second thing that you noticed were the large radiators dispersed around the dark club, heating up the place. They were large propane radiators, the kind that would typically be found outside on the patio of a restaurant. I'm sure they were a fire hazard and illegal for indoor use.

This place was a shithole. It's where Anna had come to work when she'd been kicked out of the first club we'd worked at. I'd continued working there, and now I was grateful that I hadn't followed her. But now, here I was. Fucking Alex, fuck him, I thought.

The bartender was a creep. Every night when Anna and I came in, he greeted us with a "Hi Canadaaaa," and then proceeded to ogle us in a sinister way. The sort of people that came in were not your standard mix of young partiers and older businessmen. It was primarily creepy guys who thought they could get away with inappropriate touching. And it clearly worked sometimes; one of the middle-aged dancers told

Anna all about the "dates" she'd go on with men she met at the club. She didn't always sleep with them, she insisted. I was not one to judge. I'd already found myself treading water far deeper than I'd ever wanted to jump in.

Lady Labia

"Well, she's an outtie anyways, so..." the dancer in front of me cackled, mocking one of the other dancers to a regular customer. "I've seen her in the changerooms. Trust me, she has big lips," she continued after not receiving much of a reaction. At first, I was confused about what she was even referring to. I tried my best to keep to myself where drama was concerned; some of the strippers were ruthless. Apparently, this lady felt so threatened by the other girl — who seemed to me to be a sweetheart — that she felt the need to make fun of the way her vagina looked. I later found out that sweetheart with the "outtie vagina" was dating the cackling dancer's ex.

As if women don't have enough to deal with, we're putting one another's bodies down rather than embracing them? I pondered this for a bit. It wasn't a cute look.

I didn't even know I was supposed to be insecure about my vagina lips.

The Daily Grind

Our days consisted of sleeping in until the afternoon, eating something, showering, and cracking open a drink. Anna and I would always start drinking and do our makeup before leaving to take the bus and train to our work. Ron did his own thing during this time, but we'd usually hang out a bit during the afternoon, and he'd often join us for a drink or two.

It became a cycle, dark and depressing. I dreaded going into work, and the money I made was barely worth it. Rather than making $500 on any given night, now I was barely breaking $300 on a good night. It was getting to the point where I was struggling to pay for groceries. Alcohol was my priority: without it, I couldn't work.

"I think we need to ask Mike and Josh if they have our money." I broached the idea to Anna. We'd both been struggling, and we'd both lent funds that, when returned, would get us a day or two ahead.

"Yes, they've had enough time working on Maggie Island to make money by now," she agreed, nodding slowly. "We could really use it..."

Wolf Creek

"Two young girls like yourselves oughta be careful!" a regular customer warned us. Anna and I had been telling him about our hopes to see more of the country. We explained that we'd done the East Coast with a group of friends, and wanted to see northern Australia and as much of the West Coast as possible. "If you ever feel like you hit somethin' in your car, don't stop to check," he continued ominously. "That's how people get ya, especially women… It's been known to happen where they throw things in front of the car." I was shocked, and although the club was dark, I'm sure my face gave away the horror I felt.

I know that Wolf Creek — a film in which three backpackers travelling in Australia are hunted and tortured by a sadistic serial killer — is fictional, but I recalled that the story was loosely based on real murders. On our cruise, Anna and I had gotten into a conversation with two older ladies about our adventures. They'd told us about Ivan Milat, otherwise known as "The Backpacker Murderer," who was convicted of killing two men and five women. He would pick up his victims on the side of the highway, pretending to offer them a ride. All of this was between 1989 and 1993; he was subsequently caught, charged, and convicted.

I later learned of another infamous killer, Bradley John Murdoch, who was convicted of murdering a backpacker in 2001. Unlike Ivan Milat, he was still alive, serving his sentence in Northern Australia.

Hearing a blatant warning from a local Aussie, on top of these real-life Wolf Creek stories, reminded me that I needed to be careful. This was even more vital when travelling northern parts of the country and the West Coast, because everything was so isolated and remote. Most places between Sydney and Cairns, on the other hand, were bustling with action, giving me a sense of security — however real or perceived it may have been.

I decided to look into travelling the West Coast in a similar manner to how we'd done the East Coast: with a group of other backpackers.

Walking the Straight and Narrow

Ron got by working for a marketing company for a few weeks at a time. He made decent money, and was frugal enough to live and travel off that for a couple of months. It was impressive, really. He told us that the company was looking for people to work for a couple of weeks in Melbourne, that the work was easy — it just involved standing on your feet all day. I welcomed the idea of wearing running shoes instead of high heels. I was happy to walk the straight and narrow, especially if it meant wearing comfortable shoes.

I was in. It sounded like a good gig. We'd be making over $20 an hour and working full days. It certainly beat going into the club. Anna was interested, too, but wanted to work some shifts at the club as well for extra cash.

Whenever anyone asked about what I did for work from that moment on, I always said I did "promo work," which was true. I just happened to leave out the fact I also took my clothes off for money, or explain that the promo job I'd had was all of two weeks long.

Canberra, Round 2

"I'll let you know how the club is," I told Anna as we got off the train in Canberra. She was going back to the club that I'd been kicked out of, and I was going to a new club in a different industrial area. She had booked a bed in a hostel, but I wouldn't be joining her. My new club had lodging in the back for the dancers. The website explained that they had bedrooms, a kitchen, showers, and laundry facilities. The girls who wanted to were able to stay there in between shifts, free of charge. It sounded too good to be true.

I took an Uber and found myself happily chatting with my driver. When we arrived at a large industrial building, he asked if I was sure this was the right place. It was clear that it was a strip club, and I suddenly felt self-conscious, despite our good chat. I confirmed my destination, thanked him, and wheeled my luggage through the entrance.

When I walked into the dark club, I saw a huge room with a main stage and a smaller stage off to the side. There were a couple of dance rooms to the side, and a large bar. It looked like a clean establishment. A man greeted me by the name Amber before showing me around. He took me through the club to the back, where there was a huge dressing room with rows of seats and vanity mirrors, adorned with bulbs around them — old-Hollywood style. Also in the back were a living area, two nice walk-in showers, and a small kitchenette area with everything you'd need to make meals. The man then led me into a hallway, where there were six bedrooms with bunk beds.

"There's a combination lock on the doors so that the girls feel comfortable leaving their things inside," he explained to me. "It's a no-touching club," he added. I wasn't sure if this meant I'd make no money, since I'd begun associating inappropriate touching with more take home cash.

As I got to know the owner and managers, I came to the conclusion this was by far the best club I'd ever worked at. They seemed to genuinely care about their girls, both in terms of safety and comfort. Living there was, in some ways, a breath of fresh air.

Mercedes

Most of the dancers who worked at the club slept over on weekends, when it was busiest. I found that Mercedes was the only other dancer who stayed over the two days they were closed. With straightened dark hair cut into a very emo style with choppy side bangs, and covered head to toe in colourful tattoos, she was someone I wouldn't have naturally gravitated towards. She had a very hard outward appearance, which I found intimidating. Since the two of us were the only ones there, however, we began talking, and I learned that she was kind and quite brilliant.

"I have a few rental properties already," she explained to me about her investments, "but I want to buy more. I'm on my way to becoming a millionaire." She seemed nonchalant, and I believed her. She told me that she'd been working at the club five days a week for a couple years, and was investing wisely so that she could retire from this career. She was twenty-nine years old.

I found it funny when we got private dances together with customers, because we looked completely opposite. I'd been told I looked innocent and cute, and she looked like a badass biker chick. Maybe that was part of the appeal: the angel and devil all at once.

Dealer

There was a group of guys in their early twenties who often hung out at the club. They had a designated area they sat in, off to the side of the bar. Since I was working five nights a week, we eventually began talking. They seemed easygoing, but were sometimes as unenthused as I was about being there.

I later found out that they were dealing drugs out of the club. Everything made a lot more sense after I discovered this. We were all there on business, not pleasure.

One of them was a shorter guy named Brandon. He had pouty lips and buzzed hair. "Can I buy you a drink?" he asked one night.

"Sure, thanks!" I replied. It was a quiet night, and I welcomed the alcohol and the company. We sat and started chatting. From that day on, whenever things were slow, I went to sit with the dealer crew.

Steph

"Have you seen Stephanie?" a customer asked me, clearly inebriated but searching for a dancer who'd made a positive impact on him.

"Sorry, who?" It was a busy weekend at the club, and I was only familiar with a few of the girls. On weekends, dancers came from all over, often flying in just to work a few nights. Pair that with the reality that we knew each other by our real names rather than our stage names, and I was lost.

"She has curly red hair, and she's super chill," he continued, hoping that his description would clarify things for me.

"Sorry, I don't know her," I said, and wished him luck finding her within the hectic club.

"I'm Steph," one of the dancers introduced herself. I quickly realized that this was the dancer that the guy had once asked me about. She was short and pale, with dark hair dyed a bright cherry red. She must have curled it on the night with that patron, because it was smooth and straight as she stood in front of me.

We began talking, and I found out a lot about her. She was a kindergarten teacher in Sydney, and did this for extra cash. She travelled here to dance on weekends to ensure her privacy and keep her day job. Over the course of my time stripping, I found out that a lot of the dancers had day jobs, working nine-to-fives and moonlighting for extra income. Steph told me she'd gone overboard with spending when she first got credit cards, so she had massive amounts of debt. She also wanted to pay off her car in full. I admired her. As we spoke, it became clear that she was level-headed, and while she tried to make the best out of her nights at the club, was able to balance her life outside of stripping. She used her money wisely — something I was unable to do.

Inspiration in the Most Unlikely of Places

"What would you do?" the man asked me. He was attractive, with salt and pepper creeping into his dark brown hair. He sat across from me and looked into my eyes with pain and earnestness. "If you could do anything," he continued, "what would you like to do with your life? What would make you the most happy?" I knew the answer immediately, but

I also felt self-conscious. I thought it would sound stupid coming from a girl dressed in lingerie and stripper heels, with a full face of makeup. "Angelica, the girl over there, told me she'd like to design video games," he revealed, probably hoping to show me that everyone had dreams of their own, and that he'd gotten other dancers to answer his question.

"Honestly," I began, looking at him and deciding that I had nothing to lose, "I would like to write a book." It felt good telling him the truth. I'd always had the desire to write a book and get it published, as silly as it might have sounded. It was the single unwavering item on my bucket list.

No one in any of my strip clubs had ever asked me what I wanted out of life, or about my goals. Many of them had spoken about my plans to "get out" of the industry, or had asked why I was there, but none had seemed to listen openly and reserve judgment, until this man.

He came in occasionally and carried with him a heavy sadness. It floated around him and consumed him. I never found out what he'd been through, but I could tell that he'd been cut deeply by a loss that stole the light from his eyes. His dark eyes resembled those of a wounded animal: full of compassion, but hopeless for his own future. Maybe even scared. Perhaps he wanted to give others the hope that he couldn't manage to give himself. I think of him from time to time, and I hope he has found peace.

Money Talks

I counted my money, carefully tucking the bills back into my wallet. I was shocked and ecstatic. $1760. I made that in a single shift. It was the most I'd ever made in one night. I had gotten into the habit of tucking my wallet underneath my pillow when I went to sleep in the club lodging so that whoever I shared a room with wouldn't get any wise ideas about making extra money. I was paranoid, but I had reason to be. It was a competitive environment, and it was best to be smart.

A blonde stripper was twirling around the pole on the small side stage. It was a stage I'd never seen used before, one that dancers could use if they wanted, without any required stage time. This dancer had long bleach-blonde hair, large fake breasts, and a neon green bikini. She seemed to be having the time of her life. I'd never met her before, and I learned she flew in occasionally to work at this club, otherwise staying away for months at a time.

"Woo!" she exclaimed, and then chuckled with delight as she did some maneuvers on the pole. It was a particularly quiet evening, without many customers or dancers. I found out her name was Jewel, which I thought suited her well. She shone brightly and had a huge personality.

I was chatting with a guy at a seat near her, half-watching her practice on the pole. She got off and began talking with his friend, and the next thing I knew we were all heading to a private dance room. There were three guys, so the third one picked out a girl as well: a gorgeous, thin black dancer.

The six of us were in the danceroom all together. Jewel got the bartender to start bringing us drinks; I didn't even know this was something the club offered. I imagine she tipped him for the favour. After ordering drinks and rounds of shots, she'd nonchalantly state that it would be added onto the patrons' bill. It was unbelievable, the way she did things and they simply accepted it. She was in complete control. I was in awe.

"Wanna see my party trick?" she asked with a sly grin. Everyone agreed, and she began flapping her vagina lips along to a weird voice she gave it, narrating as if it was a cartoon character. "I can make my vagina talk!" she screamed, and started laughing.

We danced for a bit. Eventually, the guy who had chosen the third girl said he couldn't afford more dances, so the two of them left. The four of us stayed for a while longer. That was how I made the $1760.

Footy Team

"It's gonna be a crazy night, girls. I hope you're all ready to make some money!" the managers told us. Apparently a local footy team was going to be coming in, and they were there to celebrate. I didn't really care what the event was, so long as it meant I'd be getting dances and making money.

I'd just invested in new lingerie for work: a ruby red bra, thong, and garter set with numerous metal clasps that cinched around my waist. It was a sexy outfit, and I was hoping the return would make the initial steep payment worthwhile.

Young men flooded the club, and I chatted with a table of them. "The things I'd do if I wasn't married," one man said. He was far older than the rest of the guys, likely their coach. I know that alcohol lowers inhibition; it's the main reason I felt the need to drink every night I worked. I also know that it makes people say things without thinking. But when the coach made that particular comment, I almost had to hold in my laughter. Whether or not he was married, nothing would change. I was there to make money, and they were there to be entertained. It was as simple as that.

Baby Belly

Anna had begun working with me at the club in Canberra because she didn't want to pay for the hostel anymore. She came up to me on a busy weekend shift with tears in her eyes. "A guy just asked me if I recently had a baby," she said, "because of my stomach."

I was speechless, but not surprised. We'd both put on weight since getting to Australia, and the constant excessive drinking didn't help. Anna was a petite girl, but most of her weight went directly to her stomach, which now had a little squishy pouch. My stomach, on the other hand, was hard and swollen, and my thighs and ass were massive. I had definitely put on more weight than her, but I was also far taller, and it was more evenly dispersed over my entire body. "Fuck him," I finally said.

ATM Machine

If anyone has seen Hustlers, they would know how easy it is to swindle intoxicated people. The reality is, a lot of strippers make money by targeting the customers who are out of it and getting dances and tips from them. I observed this behavior in a dancer dressed as a young girl, complete with pigtails and an outfit similar to Britney Spears' in her music video for Hit Me Baby One More Time, with a short school-girl skirt and a light pink crop top revealing her belly. She made numerous trips throughout the night to the club's ATM machine with a gentleman who was clearly struggling to remain standing. At one point, I couldn't help but watch as they spent a solid ten minutes at the machine, until he was finally able to withdraw the funds for more dances.

To me, there were numerous things wrong with this picture. The idea of dressing as a sexy young school girl was disgusting to me. It wasn't the first time I'd seen this in the club; many girls lied about their age, saying they'd just turned legal age to strip, despite being years older. Society's fixation on youth as desirable goes way too far, telling us that we hold value in an appearance that we lose as we age.

I also didn't like seeing this man being taken advantage of. I knew that I shouldn't care, and that this proved just how bad of a stripper I was, but I felt for him. I don't know what he was going through or what his finances looked like, but I don't imagine that he woke up, checked his bank statement, and felt content with his decisions after this evening.

Plans

I was sitting in my room at Camille's, looking at flights home to Canada. Most one-way tickets were over $1000, but I was able to find a deal for less than $800. It wasn't until afterwards that I realized I'd be flying the long way home. I pressed a few buttons, typed in my credit card information, and secured myself a flight home for a couple of months away.

I'd been scouring the Facebook Backpacker page for a potential group to travel the West Coast with. All the talk about how dangerous it was to do it alone had scared me out of our previous idea of renting or buying a car to explore on our own. To be honest, Anna's driving scared me just as much as any potential predator.

I'd come across a guy who had posted a trip, saying there were a few spots left. Apparently he'd renovated an old bus into a camper van, and did trips around the country. He primarily followed the West Coast, and would be doing a two week trip from Exmouth to Perth. He wasn't local, but his girlfriend was, and she'd be travelling with us. This gave me some comfort. Anna and I had contacted him, securing our spots for a few weeks away.

Since we'd been working and had managed to save a small chunk of money, we decided to fly to Perth first and explore. Next, we'd be flying up to Darwin for a mini vacation, where we'd make our way on a bus down to Exmouth to start the two-week trip back to Perth.

I'd booked my flight out of Perth back to Canada. That's when Anna and I would part ways, after being together almost constantly for over ten months.

Perth

As soon as we stepped out of the airport, I felt a change of pace on the West Coast. I'm sure everything that others had told me impacted my perception, but it was all true: everything felt slower and calmer here.

Anna and I waited for our Uber, and I was overcome with a wave of serenity that I hadn't experienced for a while. I didn't have to dance anymore. I had enough money to travel for two months and fly home.

We paid for our short stay at a new hostel downtown, where we would be sharing a room with about eight other people. We unloaded our things and claimed a bunk, then made our way into a common area and opened up our laptops to decompress after travelling all day.

"Should we ask Ron if he wants to holiday with us in Darwin?" I was surprised to hear Anna ask. While we were living together at Camille's, the two of them had gotten into an argument. I was definitely on Ron's side and had watched Anna screw him over. Since then, I'd chosen to see past my own issues with Anna because I didn't want to let her ruin my remaining two months in Australia. Her selfish behaviour, however, had pushed me to buy my flight home.

"We can definitely invite him, if you're both okay with it," I responded, wondering how he'd feel about meeting up with us after everything.

We messaged him, letting him know our plans for travelling and welcoming him to meet up with us. To my delight, he responded saying he'd love to join us on our journey.

Darwin

Anna and I spent a day alone in Darwin before Ron joined us. She mysteriously fell "ill" hours before he arrived, opting to stay in bed, and leaving the two of us to explore on our own. I wondered if she was self-aware enough to realize she did this every time she felt bad about her actions, rather than confronting them head on. We all have our own coping mechanisms, I thought to myself.

Sausages

A few days later, Anna was up to joining us. As I stepped outside of the air-conditioned hostel, my entire body swelled in the heat. It was unrelenting. I felt like I could barely bend my fingers, which had turned into swollen sausages. I pictured myself cracking an egg on the pavement, wondering how quickly it would cook.

Anna and I walked for a while to explore, naively thinking it would be like other cities we'd explored in Australia. While we were walking, and I was getting lightheaded, we passed some men working on a roof, their skin tanned and their bodies lean. I wondered how anyone could work in this punishing heat.

I almost fainted when we finally got to a luxurious country club, where we stumbled in and begged for a cup of ice-cold water. I came to the conclusion that my body was not built for extremes.

"I'm gonna try it," I said to Anna and Ron. We'd come to an evening market right beside the oceanfront beach. There was an assortment of food trucks selling different treats. I'd discovered one that sold crocodile meat in different forms. They urged me to tell them what it tasted like, with no desire to try it themselves. "Well, I've already had kangaroo, so I just feel like I need to try this before I leave, too," I stated, as if I needed to explain my choice.

I opted for a crocodile hot dog. The meat was white, and when I bit into it, I was underwhelmed. Unlike the kangaroo, it didn't have much taste at all.

Crocosaurus Cove

Located directly beside our hostel was Crocosaurus Cove, an attraction where you could feed baby saltwater crocodiles off a fishing line, watch crocs swim in their contained tanks, or pay an additional fee to be lowered into their tank in a transparent "Cage of Death."

The three of us decided to check it out, since it was conveniently located a matter of steps from where we were staying. Upon arriving, we were told that it was too late to sign up to go into the Cage of Death, which we quickly accepted. We were too cheap to shell out the cash anyways.

On our tour, we saw two massive crocodiles swimming around a tank. One of them was a female, who had killed all males who they'd tried putting into the tank with her. A badass bitch, I thought. Apparently her current tankmate was the first one she'd accepted and deemed worthy to live in the same vicinity as her. He was missing a leg.

"Crocodiles can slow their heart rate down to about two to three beats per minute if needed," a lady announced to us, pointing out the male croc. "This guy probably got into a fight with another male, over a female mate or food source, leading to his injury." Fighting over a female. I repeated the phrase to myself and thought about how all species were the same. "He was able to find a safe space to lay in hiding while he healed up, slowing down his heart rate so that he didn't bleed out in the meantime." Holy shit. That's incredible.

West Coast

"Until we meet again!" Ron hugged Anna and me goodbye. He would be flying back to Sydney while we were hopping on our bus to Exmouth. I was sad to be leaving Ron. He was one of the most genuine people I'd met. Mostly, though, I was just trying to stay focused on what was right in front of me: the West Coast, and then returning to whatever life awaited me back in Canada.

The drive was long, and the bus full. Anna and I slept and looked out the window at the barren land. The ground was mostly dried clay, and the trees looked like they were out of Le Petit Prince, almost ethereal in a way. Many Indigenous Australian people boarded and got off in seemingly desolate locations — heading where, I didn't know. I wondered what everyone's stories were. While Anna and I tried our best, it was difficult to ignore the pungent body odour that pervaded the vehicle. When we finally reached Exmouth, I was elated to no longer be aboard the stuffy bus.

Shark Bay

There were a total of eight of us traveling the West Coast together in the renovated camper van. This included Lisa and Cody, the couple who were running the tour. "We originally renovated a bus in New Zealand and travelled around with our friends that way," Cody explained. "We wanted to transport the bus here, since it was so much work to renovate. But it proved to be too difficult, so we just bought a new bus here and started all over again," he finished. Lisa was from a town on the West Coast that we'd be passing through towards the end of our journey. Cody was from England.

This crew was far different than the group we'd travelled with on the East Coast. We learned quickly that they didn't care for drinking, and that they wanted to do as much physical activity as possible. While I didn't join in the kitesurfing for fear of the wind taking me into the air — something that has been known to happen, I was told I was down to snorkel just about anywhere.

A few days prior, we'd done an organized snorkel tour where we swam among hundreds of reef sharks, a sting ray, and lots of coral. We decided we could do it ourselves; it hadn't seemed difficult. The guy running the tour simply swam ahead, while the rest of us followed.

This time, Cody parked the bus along the coastline, high up on a cliff. The view was gorgeous. We climbed up onto the roof to soak it in. "Wanna go check it out?" Cody suggested first. We were in. Lisa decided to nap while the rest of us ventured out, our bathing suits on and our goggles and snorkels in tow.

I followed my friends down the cliff, where we created our own path over the rough terrain, insistent on making it to the water. Looking out at the ocean, we could tell that the water was shallow for a ways, and then dropped off drastically, changing from light to deep blue.

We all waded into the water, and I dunked underneath after securing my goggles onto my face. The visibility is awful, I thought to myself, barely able to see more than a foot in front of me. Cody decided to stand on the ledge of the cliff, promising to alert us to any fish or stingrays he saw. It wasn't long before he yelled out, "There, a stingray!" and jumped in the water to join us as we swam after it.

I got this sinking feeling deep in my gut that something was wrong. It was an ominous feeling, but I tried my best to shrug it away. You're always so paranoid, I thought, and for what?

Not a minute later, Cody yelled out to us again. "There's a shark!" I looked up to see a fin circling us. "Everyone get together!" he instructed. As the shark began swimming in a smaller circle, only Cody and Brad, the other guy in our group, stayed together. I saw all the girls rushing for the shore, and I made the split second decision to do the same.

The water was so shallow that I alternated between swimming as quickly as I could and running until I fell down. The fin was now coming directly for us. I saw one of the girls in our group turn back to join Cody and Brad. Anna and I were still about neck and neck. When the water was shallow enough, I stood up with it at my ankles and looked out at the scene. The shark was turning around to head back to my three friends who'd remained in the water. It was swimming straight for them.

That's when I realized that we were in the middle of nowhere, without cell service, hours from the nearest hospital. And that's only if we could even lift an injured person up the cliffside, which was unlikely given that our two strongest people were in the ocean with the shark.

The four of us stood at the water's edge and watched in silence as our friends lowered their goggles over their eyes and dunked under the water in a huddled hug. The shark got about one meter from them before it veered off course, heading for the depths. Everyone cheered.

"It was a hammerhead," Cody told those of us not close enough to see for ourselves. "About four meters long. I just kept thinking, 'I hope it bites me instead of them. I brought them here.'" We assured him that we all had the same thoughts about ourselves. I'm not sure I was being truthful, though.

When I told my mom about the incident, she was livid. "A week before coming home! Imagine!" In hindsight, we should have known better. The place was called Shark Bay, after all.

Innocence

Once we arrived in Perth, everyone dispersed, now on their own journeys. I was the only one of the group going home. One of the girls was going to Thailand to take scuba diving courses, hoping to eventually teach it herself. The girl who'd swum back to see the shark up close had found a large camper van online that needed to be transported to Melbourne. She was going to drive it there for its new owners as a mode of free transportation. One of the guys was going to jump on another bus tour of Australia. I was the most envious of him, because it sounded like a crazy experience where he'd get to meet tons of new people.

Overall, though, I was longing to be home. I missed my family. I missed order and having a space of my own. I'd been living out of my suitcase for just under a year. I looked forward to the comforts of home: bubble baths, clean sheets in my own room, and the ability to sit around with my family and laugh.

The girls had decided to get together for one last hurrah at Little Creatures, a brewery just outside of Perth. Anna and I had taken the train to get there, but almost missed the train going back. We'd purchased one-way tickets and hadn't had the time to pay for our return trip. We thought it would be fine, that no one would be checking for tickets. This was something we'd done many times in Melbourne on public transportation, a silly means of saving money, and something we always got away with.

"Tickets," a man in a security uniform demanded. Anna and I had seen him coming. We had watched in silence as he'd scanned the other passengers' tickets until he'd finally reached us.

"Oh, here," Anna said. She handed him her ticket from the previous ride, feigning innocence. She maintained her composure while he glanced at it.

"This was from earlier today," he responded. "It's a one-way ticket." He looked at her without much expression on his face. I was getting nervous. I was flying out of the country in a matter of days; I didn't have the funds to cover any fees I might incur. I kicked myself for not buying a round trip ticket originally, thinking I'd save a few extra bucks.

"Oh." Anna looked perplexed, as if she truly thought she'd handed him a valid ticket. "I'm sorry, we're from Canada," she continued, as if that explained away our ignorance. "We just got here, like, a week ago. Do you want to see our passports?"

The security guard nodded in agreement. I rifled through my purse to find my passport and handed it over. He carefully examined our photos. I don't know if he saw the date of entry into the country. If he did, he didn't let on. "Okay, well, next time you need to buy a ticket. You may still have to pay when you leave the station on your way out." The man shrugged off the whole ordeal, accepting that we were two dumb girls travelling abroad, and moved along to the next passengers.

When we left the train station and walked through the turnstiles, we each began to run. I was sure to hold my beer carefully in my arms.

Homeward Bound

Although I flew the long way home, I chose to view it as an opportunity to get to see more of the world. I ended up in the same place with more stories to tell than if I had gone the direct route. I'm more than okay with that.

During my layover, I was sitting down and just finished video chatting with Mike. I shut my laptop and noticed a black duffle bag a row over, unattended. Shortly after, security came up to inspect it. A young man, around my age walked up and began explaining that it was his bag, and not to worry. Security left, and he turned to the young man beside him, "Oh my gosh, I hadn't even thought about it. I just went to get a snack. They asked if I had explosives!"

The other guy laughed, and they began talking about how excited they were to be going home.

"I can't wait to be home. The first thing I'm going to do when we get to Canada is have some Tim Hortons," one of them said.

I laughed and joined the conversation. "It will be nice to go home."

Empowering or Powerless?

Some people argue that stripping is empowering, that women are taking back the power that men have held for so long. Others say that it's demoralizing and shameful, that women are reinforcing stereotypes by placing their bodies in the male gaze. I can say that my own truth lies somewhere in between.

There were moments where I felt empowered and sexy. There were moments when I felt disgusting and used. I had conversations that were shallow and meaningless, and some that I'll take with me forever. Some people shared their hearts with me, and some shared their drinks. The variety of experiences I had, like the people who walked into those clubs, was as vast as the sea. It opened my eyes and mind to the similarities and differences that we share as humans. We all just want connection and love.

La Fin

Who am I? I'm your neighbour, your niece, your sister, your daughter… I am any woman and no woman. It doesn't matter who I am, it matters what I've been through. I thought it was time to share my story.

People like when things are neat and tiny: an ending neatly wrapped up with a bow. Black and white thinking, right and wrong, good and evil. But life isn't like that. Life is messy, and most things don't fit in neat little boxes. Life is a kaleidoscope of colours, including many shades of grey. And for every colour, there's a pair of stripper heels in your size.

www.ingramcontent.com/pod-product-compliance
Lightning Source LLC
LaVergne TN
LVHW021119080426
835510LV00012B/1756